fabjob *Guide to*

BECOME A
PROFESSIONAL
GOLFER

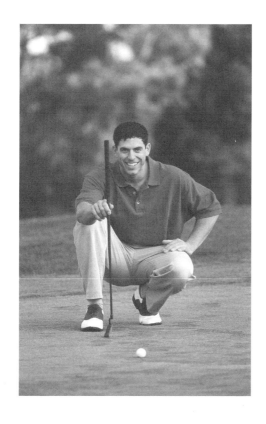

LINDA PARKER

FABJOB® GUIDE TO
BECOME A PROFESSIONAL GOLFER
by Linda Parker

ISBN 1-894638-47-6

FabJob.com Ltd.
3805 Point McKay Road NW
Calgary, Alberta, Canada T3B 4V7

4603 NE University Village, #224
Seattle, Washington, USA 98105

www.FabJob.com

About the Author

Linda Parker is an author, educator, and business consultant with a unique background in the golf industry. As a VP with the senior management team at a golf complex in Orlando, Florida, she helped develop and operate one of America's finest golf facilities, which includes a comprehensive golf education program and tournament quality courses.

As an executive in the golf industry, she worked closely with professionals in all areas of the business, including golf education, equipment development, tournament play, and with the United States Golf Association.

Linda Parker combined her background in education with her experience in the golf industry to write the *FabJob Guide to Become a Professional Golfer*. This unique book includes insider tips from players, instructors, tournament officials, and equipment designers. It is one of the most comprehensive books currently available for a golfer seeking to break into the game as a professional or to find a career niche in the world of golf. The guide is fact-filled, and rich with stories, quotes, and perspectives you can only get if you are allowed within the inner circles of the game.

The author is a graduate of the University of Kentucky. Never very far from a golf course, she and her husband, PGA Tour Veteran, Bobby Cole reside in Florida. Bobby Cole is the winner of the British Amateur, and 22 professional tournaments, including the Buick Open, the South African PGA Championship, two-time winner of the South African Open, the Seattle-Everett Open, and The World Cup of Golf (both individual and team). With more than 150 cuts and a tournament win, he is a lifetime member of the US PGA Tour.

Ms. Parker's most recent book, *The San of the Kalahari*, introduces the young reader to the Bushmen and the wonders of the Kalahari Desert.

Contents

1. Life as a Professional Golfer

1.1 Play Golf for a Living; Skip Work for the Rest of Your Life

Put yourself in the following scene:

> The sun on your shoulders feels warm and good, but not hot. There is a slight breeze, gentle and pine-scented. Butterflies dance nearby and the sky has that particular look of endless blue that always leaves you feeling as if you are far away from anything that might be wrong in the world today.

You spent last night at one of the country's most beautiful re-sort hotels. You started your morning with a short workout on the practice range and a few minutes around the greens. Now it is time for you to really get to work.

There's no checking in with the boss because you are the one in charge. So you listen for the routine of familiar sounds – the chirping of birds, the announcement of your name and the round of applause as the Starter says, "Ladies and Gentlemen, now on the tee from Any Town, USA is _____" (Just fill in the blank with your name.)

If you are considering a career in professional golf – consider this: Your place of business would be the golf course and the practice range. You would never be stuck behind a desk or in an office cubicle, and your job description – well, you get to write that yourself.

Golf is one of a limited number of professional sports where you, as the professional athlete, can do much to control your future. In golf, a weak head coach, or the fact that you did not grow up to be six foot ten never holds you back. Opportunities to compete are incredible for both male and female golfers of all ages.

Best of all, as the prize winnings printed in the sports pages show, if you play well, you can quite possibly become a millionaire or multi-millionaire along the way. From tournament winnings alone, over 200 players win in excess of $100,000 in any one playing season on the PGA Tour. The Nationwide Tour adds another 50 players to that list and the Champions Tour increases it by about 90 more. Each year approximately 70 players win over a million dollars apiece from play on the PGA or Champions Tours.

1.2 The Evolution of Professional Golf

Professional golf in today's world is not the same sport that the late Sam Snead or Ben Hogan or even Jack Nicklaus and Arnie Palmer started out to play. The great players who built tournament golf in America did not play on manicured golf courses that are the standard now. They played fairways that bore the damages of weather, insects, and disease and on greens that never saw hybrid turf grass or daily inspections by an agronomist.

As recently as the 1960's professional players traveled between tournaments more by car than by plane or personal jet. If they drove all night and teed off at eight AM, that was just part of the game. And unless they managed to win most of the tournaments in which they played, they probably spent their off season – not just practicing – but working their second job, in order to have enough money to go back out there next season and play again.

Sam Snead won over 80 PGA Tour events between 1936 and 1965, with hundreds of top five and top ten finishes. He won the Masters three times, the PGA Championship twice and the British Open once. His prize money from all of his PGA Tour tournament winnings combined, totaled a yearly earnings average of only $20,000. Arnold Palmer won less money from his entire career in PGA Tour play – a total including more than 60 Tour wins – than Tiger Woods made in his first full year in professional golf.

As you can see, the sport has changed. While golf today is both competitive and demanding, it is also a game of tremendous opportunities.

Determination and your willingness to work hard can help you achieve your goal. Add good advice like the valuable suggestions you'll find in this guide, and the game you love could become the career of a lifetime. When all of the factors come together, it is clear why professional golfers say,

> *"Play golf for a living and never work a day in your life."*

1.3 Benefits Beyond the Prize Money

Playing professional golf means the chance to play a game you love, to earn big dollars doing it, and to possibly write your name in the pages of sports history. Such incredible rewards are certainly sufficient for most players but, in fact, the game can give you even more.

Golf is as demanding mentally as physically. Your mastered skills of concentration and disciplines of practice will reflect positively in everything you attempt throughout your life. Because of golf, you will sharpen your decision-making skills, build your courage, and over and over again, relearn humility.

You will have the privilege to share the game with other players who love it as well. As you travel from tournament to tournament, your competitors will become your friends and in a way, your family. Together you and other touring pros will see the world and share a game with a legendary heritage.

Golf will give you the opportunity to play professionally for more years than any other sport. Long after you have stopped competing, you will enjoy spending time on the fairway for the sunshine, the exercise, and the pleasure of seeing that little white ball drop in the hole again.

But perhaps the single greatest reward of the game is that every round begins with a new scorecard. Each time you walk onto the course, you play with the prospect that it is your day to be a champion.

If this sounds like the career of your dreams, the FabJob *Guide to Become a Professional Golfer* is the book to help get you there!

1.4 Overview of This Guide

The *FabJob Guide to Become a Professional Golfer* takes an in-depth look at the different pathways that can be followed to professional golf success.

Chapter 2, Getting Ready, covers important preliminary steps to prepare you for becoming a professional golfer. You will discover that it is never too soon – or too late – to get started. You will find the best resources for improving your skills and learning to play golf, get advice on choosing your clubs and other equipment, and gain an understanding of how the professional golf industry operates.

Chapter 3 focuses on Playing on the Major Tours. This chapter tells you what is required to compete on the major professional tours – PGA, Nationwide, Champions, and LPGA. You will learn about the prize money, who gets to play, and how beginners can break in by doing well at a National Qualifying Tournament (also known as "Q School"). You will learn what goes on behind the scenes during tournament weeks.

Chapter 4, Other Opportunities, provides information about things you can do while working your way to the top. In this chapter you will learn about developmental tours, international tours, and part-time professional golf. This chapter also shows you options for being part of the world of professional golf through related careers and internships.

Finally, Chapter 5 offers helpful advice on Your Team. You will discover how to get an agent and sponsors. You will also learn about other team members including your caddie, swing coach, fitness trainer, and sports psychologist.

And throughout the guide, you will find the stories of actual players, their struggles, their successes, and the insider tips that most of them had to learn the hard way. This comprehensive book explains all the things your father would have told you, if only he had been a member of the PGA Tour.

2. Getting Ready

Chapter 2 teaches you many of the things you will need to do to prepare for a career as a professional golfer. You will discover what qualities successful pro golfers have and how to develop those qualities yourself. You will learn about the pro golf lifestyle, schools that can improve your golf skills, and the equipment and clothing you will need.

This chapter also provides an overview of how the world of professional golf operates including rules, golf organizations, and a look at the Majors. When you are finished with this chapter, you will have an understanding of what it takes to succeed in this career, and how to get started.

2.1 It is Never too Soon – or Too Late – to Get Started

2.1.1 Early Successes

Who hasn't seen photos of Tiger Woods at the age of two, with his scaled-down golf club in hand? He shot a nine-hole score of 48 by the time he was three. By the age of five, he had already been featured in Golf Digest. At 18, he won the US Amateur, becoming that tournament's youngest winner. And at 21, he set the record as the youngest Masters Tournament Champion ever.

In another part of the world, Spain's Sergio Garcia did not take up the game of golf until the age of three. At 14, Sergio set a record as the youngest player to make the cut in a European Tour event and by 19, was the youngest Ryder Cup participant in history.

With such stories of youthful achievement, it might seem that only players who take up the game in their cribs stand any chance for success. But despite the publicity that youthful record-breakers gain with their accomplishments, the young player does not always dominate professional golf.

If you are not one of golf's child prodigies, do not give up. You still have time to get in the game. A look at how many years most "Youngest

Winner" records stand before they are broken, reminds us that young phenoms are the exception, not the norm.

When Tiger won the US Amateur, he set a new record as the youngest winner of that event. The title previously belonged to golfer, Robert Gardner – and it had stood since 1909 when Gardner won as a nineteen-year old competitor. When Tiger became the youngest Masters Champion, he took that honor away from Jack Nicklaus. But that record had stood since 1965. And Tiger was not the youngest Masters Tournament competitor to qualify to play all four rounds – that record, set in 1967, belongs to South African golfer, Bobby Cole.

Likewise, for all of Sergio Garcia's incredible achievements, he is not the youngest winner of a European Tour event. Another South African, Dale Hayes, holds that record with his 1971 Spanish Open win at the age of 19. Nick Faldo's record as the youngest member of a Ryder Cup Team stood for 20 years before Sergio came along to break it. Even Sergio's British Amateur win at the age of 18 years and four months did not make him that event's youngest champion. That record too, belongs to Bobby Cole, who was barely one month past his 18th birthday in 1966 when he won the British Amateur at Carnoustie, Scotland.

There are players who make impressive accomplishments at amazingly young ages. It is understandable that headlines and sports commentators focus on them. But professional tournaments are played around the world each week and the youngest players competing are seldom the winners.

Success in golf comes to different players at different ages and different stages of their games. Most often, it comes to players as they gain experience, not in the first few years of their careers.

Young golf superstars will always come along. Some of them will be able to turn their early success into outstanding lifetime careers. Others will not. They will fail to develop the combination of skills needed to continue to play well, year after year. Their names will disappear from the leader boards and their careers will exist only in faded newspaper clippings.

All professional golfers have good days and bad days, good years and bad years, at every stage of their careers. Their careers survive if they learn to accept the accomplishments of other players without losing their own confidence. They must recognize that they cannot win every tournament. Then, with astounding determination, they must go out on the golf course and try to do just that.

2.1.2 Late Bloomers

How late is too late to begin a career in professional golf? Ask Tom Lehman, Calvin Peete, Fred Funk, or Brandel Chamblee. All highly successful on the PGA or Champions Tours, they are excellent examples of golfers whose careers improved with age. None of these players achieved tournament wins on the PGA Tour until they were in their mid-thirties.

Other notable players have taken detours in their professional golf careers because of injuries, military duty, or a change of heart. Some have had games that were simply slower to peak. Particularly interesting careers include those of Ben Hogan, Jay Siegel, Joel Edwards, Tom Pernice, Jr., and Joe Durant. Both Pernice and Edwards were over 40 years old before they achieved their first PGA Tour victories. With tournament prize money now substantial, it is easier than ever for players – even late bloomers – to afford to play the Tour for years in pursuit of a win.

The Champions Tour has produced its own variety of late bloomers. This talented group includes players who had no experience on professional tours or only a few years of play on the PGA or Nationwide Tours. Players including Dana Quigley, Jim Holtgrieve, and Walter Hall have all claimed spots on the Champions Tour.

As younger men, some had pursued careers as teaching professionals while others worked in businesses unrelated to golf. All were united by a love of the game, continued practice, devotion to amateur or mini tour (developmental tour) events, and the dream that when their 50th birthday came, they would give professional golf a serious shot.

You can read more about the playing records of these and other great golfers by visiting the PGA Tour and LPGA Tour's websites, **www.pgatour.com** and **www.lpga.com** where you can search player biographies. Or, study year-by-year player histories at Golf Online, **www.golfonline.com**.

Notable Late Bloomers in Professional Golf

Tom Lehman, winner of the British Open, four PGA Tour events and four BUY.COM Tour events (then known as the Ben Hogan Tour, and now called the Nationwide Tour). Lehman played on three Ryder Cup Teams and three Presidents Cup teams. He did not win his first event on the BUY.COM Tour until he was 31, and his first PGA Tour event until he was 36.

Calvin Peete, winner of twelve PGA Tour events, with numerous top finishes on the SR PGA Tour. Peete suffered a childhood injury that left his left arm permanently damaged. He did not learn to play golf until the age of 23. Peete did not win his first PGA Tour event until he was 36 years old.

Betsy Rawls, winner of 55 LPGA Tour events, including eight majors. You cannot exactly call Rawls a late bloomer, since her first professional win came at age 23. Yet, remarkably, before turning pro she took the time to graduate Phi Beta Kappa from the University of Texas with degrees in physics and math.

Fred Funk, winner of five PGA Tour events with numerous top finishes in PGA tournaments. Funk's career path included seven years as the golf coach at the University of Maryland, and a stint in the newspaper business before he won his first PGA Tour event at the age of 36.

Brandel Chamblee, winner of one PGA Tour event, one BUY.COM Tour event with numerous top finishes on both tours. Chamblee grew up riding horses and roping calves in Texas. He taught himself the game of golf by watching players on television. His BUY.COM Tour win came at the age of 29 and Chamblee did not win on the PGA Tour until he was 36 years old.

2.1.3 Players Who Can't Be Stopped

There are a few remarkable stories of players who defy the odds (and the imagination) and win PGA Tour events both as young stars and as tour veterans. When Jack Nicklaus gave up his title to Tiger Woods, as Youngest Winner of the Masters, he still held claim to the honor of being the Oldest Winner of that tournament. He won the Masters in 1986 at the age of 46; it was his sixth Masters Championship.

Mark O'Meara, with a Masters win in 1998 at the age of 41, is the oldest first time winner of the event. He followed it that same year with a first time victory at the British Open. The two wins also earned him the distinction of being the oldest player to win the Masters and the British Open in the same year.

Gary Player has won official PGA or Champions Tour events in each of five decades. His 19th Champions Tour victory came just before his 63rd birthday, making him that tour's second oldest winner. With three British Open victories, (all in different decades) Player was the oldest player to qualify to play four rounds in that event when he played in 1995 at the age of 59. Gary Player's advice to any young player for achieving staying power and longevity in the game:

> "I credit my ability to play professionally for six decades to good health, good diet and fitness training. I began working out with weights and stretching exercises at the age of ten and I am still committed to it now in my sixties. To survive in professional golf you must love to play, you must set goals and you must avoid the number one killer of human beings – obesity."

If you are serious in your plan for a career in professional golf, take the time to read the stories of the players who have made golf great. Public libraries and most bookstores have sections devoted to the game of golf, including the biographies of notable players. After you watch tournament play on The Golf Channel (covered in section 2.6.3), stick around and watch the specials on the history of the game and the lives of veteran players. Study their stories and the strategies they use to stay in the game year after year.

Use all of these players as your teachers. Learn, by studying the lives of others, what it takes for you to become a player who builds a life-long career in professional golf – a player who can't be stopped.

2.2 Qualities of Successful Pro Golfers

You may have great golfing skills and your game may be right for professional golf. You may also have the character traits of determination and commitment to be able to maintain a lifelong career in the game. But, how do you know if the day-to-day life of professional golf is right for you?

In this section and the one that follows, you will get an overview of what is required of professional golfers. To begin, here is a list of the qualities necessary for a lifelong professional golf career. Some are physical qualities, some are mental, and others are based on knowledge or experience. Note which ones you have, and which you will need to develop. This section has basic suggestions to help you start developing specific skills; more in-depth advice and resources are offered throughout this guide.

Physical Qualities

To become a professional golfer, the physical qualities you require are:

_____   Physical stamina

_____   Skill (also described as good golf mechanics)

_____   Strength and muscle flexibility

There is a variety of ways to develop your physical qualities, including: one-on-one instruction with a coach, golf school, fitness training programs, plus plenty of practice. You will find information about coaches and golf schools later in this chapter. Also see section 5.3.2 for advice on finding a swing coach, and section 5.3.3 for advice on working with a fitness trainer and increasing and maintaining physical strength.

You may successfully train yourself by using programs in golf or fitness publications or websites. On the next two pages you will find some drills you can do to improve your skill. Section 2.4.5 offers additional advice on "Educating Yourself" and includes website information about some excellent free online resources for improving your physical skills.

Drills to Improve Your Techniques

As you practice and play, try the following three Drills to improve your techniques.

Drill I

This drill is recommended by Tommy Marino, Master Instructor at the Jim McLean Golf School at Miami's Doral Resort.

Purpose: Reinforces correct body weight shifting during the downswing.

Start Position: Place a 9-iron flat on the ground where you plan to hit your shots, with the club shaft pointed toward your target. The club head is face-up and placed toward the target, with the grip of the club located away from the target.

Stand in your normal stance for the club with which you are practicing. You may do this drill using a mid-iron (5, 6 or 7).

Place your right heel on the face of the 9-iron you placed on the ground. Your body weight on the clubface of the 9-iron will elevate the shaft of this club approximately 40 to 45 degrees from the ground surface. Keep your left foot appropriately positioned in your normal stance relative to your right foot.

Execute your backswing. If you properly shift your weight from balanced on both feet to shifted to your right foot, the shaft of the 9-iron will remain elevated. However, when you begin your down swing, using proper weight shift from predominately right foot to predominately left foot, *if you have the correct lifting of the right heel*, the shaft of the 9-iron will lower to the ground.

By impact, approximately 90% of your body weight should be on your left foot.

This drill can be done with or without a ball.

Drill II

Purpose: Reinforces keeping correct spine angle through impact.

Start Position: Stand in your set-up position, without a club in your hand, and with your heels and buttocks touching a wall.

Make your golf swing (without your club). Focus on keeping your buttocks lightly against the wall throughout both your back swing and your down swing. Concentrate on developing greater awareness of your spine angle.

Step away from the wall. Practice the same swing, this time with your club. Try to recreate the same spine angle you achieved when you were against the wall.

Remember, sometimes in golf as in life, you achieve your best when, "Your back's up against the wall!"

Drill III

Purpose: To increase the width of the placement of your hands at the top of your golf swing.

Start Position: Assume your normal set-up or address position.

With your right hand, grip your left forearm just above the wrist. You should place your right hand so that your fingers are on the bottom of your left arm and your right thumb is on the top of your left arm. Your thumb should point toward your target.

From this position make your full backswing, keeping your left arm straight. When you are at the top of your backswing, slide your right hand into your normal grip position, but without changing the position of your left hand. Execute your downswing.

This drill focuses on establishing the maximum width placement of your hands when at the top of your backswing. Wide width placement of your hands contributes to more power and club head speed. Do not be fooled by the false feeling that this is a shorter, less powerful swing.

Mental Qualities

Successful professional golfers have the following mental qualities:

_____   Ability to play under competitive pressure

_____   Commitment or perseverance

_____   Composure to rebound from errors or bad luck

_____   Confidence

To improve your ability to play under competitive pressure, play competitively whenever possible. When you cannot play in tournaments, play for money, dinner, or anything else that increases the pressure on you to play well.

To improve specific mental qualities, consult sports psychologists or read their work on techniques for improving tournament performance. Section 5.3.4 offers tips on what to look for in a sports psychologist and lists useful resources.

An article on using brain-training programs to enhance your performance begins on the next page. You might also want to investigate the GolfPsych website at **www.golfpsych.com**, where you can test yourself with a questionnaire designed to "measure your mental game."

Time management is another quality golfers must consider. Being disciplined with your time can help you avoid costly mistakes. You will likely have many tasks and events to juggle, and you don't want to miss a tournament play opportunity because you forgot to apply by the deadline.

To make the most of your time, get organized! Use calendar books, day planners, or any other organized notebook that will help you see and plan your day. It's also a good idea to invest in a small tape recorder for keeping track of great thoughts that come to you while driving between tournaments

The Golfer's Training Brain and The Performer

by Colin R. Keogh
Accelerated Excellence, Incorporated

"Golf is a game played on a six inch course –
the space between your ears!"
– Sam Snead

In the last 30 years, the training a professional golfer must go through has dramatically changed. While 90% of the game is mental and 10% physical, golfers of the past spent 90% of their time practicing the physical part of the game. With today's level of competition, a professional golfer must prepare the mind as well as the body. So was born the specialty of Sports Psychology.

It is the mind that holds the determining factors over just about all of our performances and behavior, and so it is in mastering the mind, that the golfer has the greatest chance of performing at his personal best. Back in the 1950's, the Soviet Union employed hypnotists to enhance the performance of their Olympic athletes. Over the last 50 years, the techniques have been studied and refined to allow world class athletes to achieve peak performances and sustain them through a balance of mental and physical preparation.

In order to attain this balance a golfer must understand the mental part of the game and learn how to prepare his or her conscious and unconscious brain for the stress encountered during tournaments. Let's look at how the brain works and then we will look at how to enhance your performance by using the knowledge you have gained.

Different high-level functions of your brain are localized into either the left side or the right side of the brain. The left side of your brain performs analytical activities such as: planning and goal setting, analysis of complex skills and building of images of how that skill should be performed, and self instruction or self talk. This part of your brain analyzes everything. As you are learning a skill, your left-brain examines every step for errors and makes you do it over and over until you have accomplished the skill. We will call this part of your brain, the training brain.

The right side of your brain controls complex activities such as: imagery, coordination of complex movements, and integration of skills into complex movement. This part of your brain integrates the isolated skills you learned with your training brain into one component that completes the finished skill set at the highest level. We will call this side of your brain, the performer. During different activities, you will need to stimulate different parts of you brain and also develop the network between, to both accelerate the learning process and enhance your performance.

While you are on the driving range, you want the training part of your brain to take control and analyze your swing, your head movement, and the many other mechanics of your shot. However, when you are on the course, you want your performance part of your brain to dominate. When you are in a match, you need to perform without thinking of the mechanics. If you are constantly analyzing your shots during a game, the distraction will effectively destroy the flow of your skill set and your mental state will suffer.

We have all been on the course and heard another golfer say, "I lifted my head too soon." This golfer has just made a bad shot and will have a tough time regaining his previous level of concentration because he has let his training brain take over during the match.

To enhance your training and performance you can use a new technology called brain wave entrainment. With this technology, different frequencies of sound are used to stimulate certain areas of your brain. By using this technology, you can train your training brain to elevate its activity during your practice and your performer brain to elevate its activity during the match.

You must establish balance between the body and mind. This

balance is not something we are born with, it is a process that we must go through to make sure that we are both mentally and physically prepared for the tasks we want to accomplish.

Another technology that can be exploited to enhance your game is Neuro Linguistic Programming (NLP). NLP is a modeling tool that allows the skilled practitioner to understand how excellent performers perform excellently - a set of tools and techniques that allow one to really understand processes and states that other champions go through to achieve results.

NLP is the way in which you can guide awareness, imagery, and internal experiences in a manner that allows you to experience more choices in how you perform and allows you to make changes in undesirable behaviors. When combined, Neuro Linguistic Programming and brain wave entrainment have moved to the front as the most effective way to synchronize your mind and body into a "zone" that will allow you to perform at your absolute peak.

Neuro Linguistic Programming and brain wave entrainment technology can play a major role in helping a golfer prepare himself mentally. There are many aspects of a golfer's game that can be enhanced through the combination of these technologies.

- **Feeling relaxed.** Most people believe that we must be "psyched up" to play at our best, but research shows that this is not true. When an athlete is "psyched" they let adrenalin take over and their brain does not perform at its best. The best state of arousal is slightly above normal, that is relaxed, but with a feeling of energy.

- **Self-Confidence.** In NLP we use presuppositions. Instead of saying 'I might win,' you use the statement, 'when I win'. There is no fear, and a trust in your training and abilities moves you towards success.

- **Focus.** When you are totally absorbed in the moment, there are no distractions and you have total concentration.

- **Subconscious Actions.** You have let your performance brain take over and you are on autopilot. You don't have to think or analyze, you just do. Golfers perform better when apparently no conscious thoughts are involved.

- **Control.** You feel in control, everything you have visualized happening is happening.

Through the use of NLP and brain wave entrainment you can: overcome self-doubt, increase your mental imagery, promote positive visualization, increase confidence, increase motivation, increase concentration and focus, eliminate negativity, and reduce performance anxiety. In other words you can program your brain for success.

These techniques are not a magic bullet, they will not, and cannot, turn a talent-less athlete into a superstar, however by using the combination of NLP and brain wave entrainment you can amplify your inherent talent and abilities.

Knowledge

While golf skills are essential to your success, they are not sufficient by themselves. To be successful as a professional golfer, you also need to have the following:

_____   In-depth knowledge of the rules of golf

_____   Ability to play in different types of weather

_____   Understanding of different types of courses

_____   Understanding of equipment

_____   Understanding of game strategy

There are many ways to increase your knowledge of the fine points of the game. If you are fortunate to establish relationships with skilled players, seek their advice on playing, equipment, and courses.

You can also increase your knowledge of game strategy by studying skilled professionals in play, and reading about the strategies of the superstars. You will find many recommended resources for learning more about game strategy throughout this guide. One place to start is with this excellent book: *The Methods of Golf's Masters: How They Played and What You Can Learn From Them*, by Dick Aultman, Ken Bowden, and Herbert Warren Wind.

Experimenting is another way to increase your knowledge. For example, try different equipment on the practice range or in practice rounds. Experiment with different strategies when you play for practice. Learn what will work for you under different circumstances.

As a young golfer, Gary Player was once spotted on a hot, sunny afternoon playing a South African golf course while wearing his full rain gear. When asked why he was dressed that way, Player explained that he would soon be heading for England to play in the British Open, where, he pointed out, "it rains a lot!"

Play in all types of wind, weather, and course conditions. Play when, because the weather is so unfavorable, you are the only one on the course. Likewise, to understand different types of courses, play a variety of course designs, terrains, and grass types. Visit websites of golf courses to better understand their layouts, speed of greens, and other variables. Most courses can be easily found online by searching their name, or visit the *Golf Magazine* Golf Course Guide at **www. golfcourse.com**.

Additional resources for learning golf course design are included in section 4.5.2 (golf course design is one of the "Other Golf Careers" included in this section), while section 2.4.5 gives advice on how to learn the rules of golf, and section 2.5 has detailed information about equipment.

Experience

Professional golfers quickly get experience in two additional areas:

_____ Experience playing in front of a gallery

_____ Experience playing in front of television cameras

Very few things prepare you for the experience of playing in front of a gallery, sound crews, camera crews, and with on-course commentators all around, yet the more practiced your playing skills, the less you will be affected by distractions. Practice! Play competitively or under distracting conditions whenever you have the opportunity. Work to improve your concentration skills, possibly with a sports psychologist (see section 5.3.4).

2.3 The Pro Golfer's Lifestyle

2.3.1 Quiz: Is Pro Golf for You?

Take the following short quiz. Read each statement and the three choices that follow it. Then select the choice that is closest to your reaction.

1. **There's no place like home; I always sleep best in my own bed with my favorite pillow.**

    _✓___ a. That's me, all right. It took years of hard sleeping to get that pillow molded to fit my head.

    _____ b. Home is best, but as long as the mattress is decent, I can fall asleep.

    _____ c. ZZZZZ! I can catch a good snooze anywhere, anytime.

    Fact: Professional golf means that you will spend many nights in hotels that may not be comfortable, yet each morning, you will still need to perform at your best.

2. **Honesty on the golf course is always the best policy.**

    _____ a. I disagree. I think a smart person knows when to tell the truth and when to lie creatively.

    _____ b. Maybe, but sometimes there is a fine line between fact and fiction.

    _✗___ c. I agree. The difference between the truth and a lie is black and white, at least on a golf green.

Fact: The Official Rules of Golf require you to police your own errors and those of your playing partners. You cannot be Mr. Nice Guy or let something slide. You are expected to uphold the integrity of the game. Fail to report an error and you will be penalized; cheat, and you will lose your career.

3. **I am a private person. What I do in my personal life is my own business.**

   _____ a. That describes me exactly. I expect others to get a life and stay out of mine.

   _____ b. What people say about me doesn't matter too much one way or the other.

   _____ c. Hey, As long as they talk about me, I don't care what they say!

   Fact: The press will talk about you. They will get some things wrong. And they will be there to point out every mistake you make and every weakness in your game.

4. **I've been swinging a golf club the same way for years. It may not look like Tiger's swing, but it works for me.**

   _____ a. I will never change my golf swing. It has worked so far, and I am sticking with it.

   _____ b. My golf swing feels pretty good, but there might be room for improvement.

   _____ c. I am always trying to improve my technique.

   Fact: The competition, the equipment, and your body will all change. To stay in the game, you have to be prepared to change with it.

Count your answers. If you selected C for all four questions, your personality may be perfectly suited to the life of a professional golfer. Mostly B's suggests you may have to make adjustments, but professional golf could still be a great life for you. If you selected four A's, just make sure you think through this career choice carefully before you make any big plunges.

Most people will have mixed A's, B's and C's. No set of answers (even all A's) means you have to give up your dream of being a professional golfer. But, early in your career learn as much as you can about all aspects of the lifestyle. Learn the tricks to cope with its down sides, and learn as much as you can about other careers in the golf industry – just in case you ever decide to change your plan.

2.3.2 Reality Check – Life on the Road

Life as a tour player means hotels, airports, restaurants, and laundromats. Tour life means you have a sixty-pound, fully loaded golf bag that accompanies you everywhere. Everything else you need, from clothes to personal items to your paperwork to enter the next tournament, must fit in the fewest number of suitcases possible – preferably one.

During the first two weeks you play on a tour, you will realize you have eaten forty-two consecutive meals in restaurants, where all of the menus seem to be the same. Moreover, you will have that nagging thought that you are an athlete in training – you are supposed to be eating a healthful diet. When your budget is calling for drive-thru tacos, your body needs fish and fresh veggies, and your taste buds are longing for mom's meatloaf, you will know you really are a professional golfer on tour.

And a warning to hay fever sufferers. PGA Tour events begin their season each year in Hawaii and Florida, then work their way through California and across the South. They follow warm weather, flowers in bloom and what some golfers call the Pollen Trail.

If you choose to try tour life, close your eyes to the inconveniences. Invest in a sturdy suitcase, with wheels that roll properly and will not snap off when you tug on it. Look for Mom and Pop diners with crowded parking lots or to buy fresh fruit, milk, and cereal at the local supermarket. It is cheaper, healthier and it is a change of pace.

And before you hit the road, schedule a visit to the allergist. There are medications available that really do help without leaving you sound asleep from the side effects. Then throw a white pillowcase or two into your luggage. Your own pillowcase – one you know has been laundered with bleach, can work wonders to improve your good night's sleep and reduces exposure to allergens in motel bedding. Besides, it makes a great laundry bag as you head to the dry cleaners.

The last word on this comes from a man who has seen many players struggling to get started in professional golf, Gary De Serrano, President of the Tight Lies Tour (one of golf's most successful mini tours), comes this observation and advice:

> "The biggest shock most players have as they begin playing on a Tour is the great number of guys who can beat them. That, and just how quickly all their laundry winds up dirty again."

To solve these problems, De Serrano advises:

> "Don't get caught up in the grumbling of players who talk about how hard things are when you are playing the Tour. Do what you came to do. Practice. Play well. Play every week. ... and have your clothes dry cleaned, they'll hold up longer."

If you're up for the lifestyle, then read on to find out how to prepare yourself by getting an education – whether at college, golf schools, or with a coach. If you're not sure if a career as a pro golfer will give you the lifestyle you want, check out section 4.1 about golf mini tours. Consider spending a season playing mini tour golf before you set your sights on a lifetime career in the game.

2.4 Getting an Education

2.4.1 Should You Go to School?

The pathways to success in professional golf are as varied as the personalities and playing styles of the golfers who follow them.

For some players, moving from high school golf to a college golf team, to the professional tours or mini tours is a good plan. Other players have found success after attending golf schools or working in a golf-related job while at the same time continuing their training and practicing. A few players complete high school, focus on one-on-one instruction with a coach, and go straight to professional play.

Whether it is best to attend school or go straight to tour play is a much-debated subject in golf. A player whose game is ready for top-level tour play but goes to college instead is missing out on potential winnings, equipment endorsements, and tournament titles. If he is strong, healthy, and highly motivated, he may be missing some of his best playing years. The collegiate player could find himself left behind by the competition.

Then there is the matter of coaches. Most college coaches are excellent, but they specialize in working with the collegiate golfer. A private instructor – perhaps one who is known for working with successful tour players – may be a better instructor for a potential superstar than the collegiate coach, who most often deals with golf as a team sport.

Both Phil Mickelson and Justin Leonard have spoken frequently to the press about how much they believe they gained from playing collegiate golf before turning pro. Yet, a look at the careers of Sergio Garcia or Ernie Els, who bypassed college and went straight to professional competition, proves that there is more than one pathway to a career as a professional golfer.

2.4.2 College Programs

Attending college before seeking a place as a touring professional has been a widespread approach to professional golf. It permits you to pursue the game and at the same time earn a college degree. Many colleges and universities have great traditions in golf. Wake Forest University is one of the most notable, with an alumni list that includes Arnold Palmer, Lanny Wadkins, Scott Hoch, Jay Sigel, Jay Haas, Curtis Strange, and many other greats of the game.

Wake Forest University

> Men's Golf
> Wake Forest University
> Athletics Department
> Box 7265 Reynolds Station
> Winston-Salem, North Carolina 27109
> Phone: 336-758-6000
> **http://wakeforestsports.fansonly.com/
> sports/m-golf/wake-m-golf-body.html**

> Women's Golf
> Wake Forest University
> Athletics Department
> Box 7265 Reynolds Station
> Winston-Salem, North Carolina 27109
> Phone: 336-758-5858
> **http://wakeforestsports.fansonly.com/
> sports/w-golf/wake-w-golf-body.html**

Some of the other large colleges or universities with well-known men's and women's golf programs include:

Auburn

Men's Golf
Athletics Department
P.O. Box 351
Auburn, Alabama 36831
Phone: 334-844-4750
Email: athletics@auburn.edu
www.auburntigers.com/mensgolf

Women's Golf
Athletics Department
P.O. Box 351
Auburn, Alabama 36831
Phone: 334-844-4750
Email: athletics@auburn.edu
www.http://www.auburntigers.com/womensgolf

Brigham Young University

Men's Golf
Brigham Young University
Provo, Utah 84602
Phone: 801-422-2096
www.byucougars.com/golf_m

Women's Golf
Brigham Young University
Provo, Utah 84602
Phone: 801-422-4225
www.byucougars.com/golf_w

Duke University

Men's Golf
Duke University
Durham, North Carolina 27708
Phone: 919-681-2494
Email: rwmyers@duaa.duke.edu
http://goduke.fansonly.com/sports/
m-golf/duke-m-golf-body.html

Women's Golf
Duke University
Durham, North Carolina 27708
Phone: 919-681-2628
Email: dsb5@dduaa.uke.edu
**http://goduke.fansonly.com/sports/
w-golf/duke-w-golf-body.html**

Oklahoma State

Men's Golf
220 Athletic Center
Oklahoma State University
Stillwater, Oklahoma 74078
Phone: 405-707-7842
www.okstate.com/sports/m-golf/okst-m-golf-frame.html

Women's Golf
220 Athletic Center
Oklahoma State University
Stillwater, Oklahoma 74078
Phone: 405-707-7844
www.okstate.com/sports/w-golf/okst-w-golf-frame.html

Stanford

Men's Golf
Department of Athletics
Stanford University
Arrillaga Family Sports Center
Stanford, California 94305
Phone: 650-323-0939
**http://gostanford.fansonly.com/sports/
w-golf/stan-m-golf-body.html**

Women's Golf
Department of Athletics
Stanford University
Arrillaga Family Sports Center
Stanford, California 94305
Phone: 650-323-0938
**http://gostanford.fansonly.com/sports/
w-golf/stan-w-golf-body.html**

The University of Arizona

Men's Golf
The University of Arizona
Intercollegiate Athletics
McKale Memorial Center
1 National Championship Dr.
PO Box 210096
Tucson, Arizona 85721
Phone: 520-621-4658
**http://arizonaathletics.fansonly.com/sports/
m-golf/ariz-m-golf-body.html**

Women's Golf
The University of Arizona
Intercollegiate Athletics
McKale Memorial Center
1 National Championship Dr.
PO Box 210096
Tucson, Arizona 85721
Phone: 520-621-5777
**http://arizonaathletics.fansonly.com/sports/
w-golf/ariz-w-golf-body.html**

UCLA

Men's Golf
UCLA Athletic Department
J.D. Morgan Center
P.O. Box 24044
Los Angeles, California 90024
Phone: 310-825-8699
**http://uclabruins.ocsn.com/sports/
m-golf/ucla-m-golf-body.html**

Women's Golf
UCLA Athletic Department
J.D. Morgan Center
P.O. Box 24044
Los Angeles, California 90024
Phone: 310-825-8699
**http://uclabruins.ocsn.com/sports/
w-golf/ucla-w-golf-body.html**

University of Florida

Men's Golf
University Athletic Association
P.O. Box 14485
Gainesville, Florida 32604
Phone: In-state 800-344-2867
Phone: Others 352-375-4683
www.gatorzone.com/golf/men

Women's Golf
University Athletic Association
P.O. Box 14485
Gainesville, Florida 32604
Phone: In-state 800-344-2867
Phone: Others 352-375-4683
www.gatorzone.com/golf/women

University of Kentucky

Men's Golf
UK Athletics
Memorial Coliseum
Lexington, Kentucky 40506
Phone: 859-257-6506
http://ukathletics.ocsn.com/sports/m-golf

Women's Golf
UK Athletics
Memorial Coliseum
Lexington, Kentucky 40506
Phone: 859-257-4861
http://ukathletics.ocsn.com/sports/w-golf

University of Nevada at Las Vegas

Men's Golf
UNLV Athletics Department
4505 Maryland Parkway
Las Vegas, Nevada 89154
Phone: 702-895-3714
http://unlvrebels.fansonly.com/sports/
m-golf/unlv-m-golf-body.html

Women's Golf
UNLV Athletics Department
4505 Maryland Parkway
Las Vegas, Nevada 89154
Phone: 702-895-2091
FAX: 702-895-0985
**http://unlvrebels.fansonly.com/sports/
w-golf/unlv-w-golf-body.html**

University of Tennessee

Men's Golf
117 Stokely Athletics Center
University of Tennessee
Knoxville, Tennessee 37996
Phone: 865-974-3834
**http://utsports.fansonly.com/sports/
m-golf/tenn-m-golf-body.html**

Women's Golf
117 Stokely Athletics Center
University of Tennessee
Knoxville, Tennessee 37996
Phone: 865-974-4275
**http://utladyvols.ocsn.com/sports/
w-golf/tennw-wgolf-body.html**

Many other colleges and universities are also good choices. Make sure, however, that they have an officially recognized golf team. You can check with the National Collegiate Athletic Association (NCAA) that governs college sports. They set and maintain the standards of fairness. The NCAA is the record keeper and the legislative body for all issues in officially sanctioned college athletic competitions. Almost one thousand colleges or universities in the US are members of the NCAA.

NCAA guidelines classify schools as Division I, II or III based on the number of men's and women's sports offered at each school, and other factors including the size of attendance at home game events. Full lists of all Division I and II teams with men's or women's golf teams are available at the NCAA website, **www.NCAA.org**. You can search this information by division, conference, or region under Schools Sponsoring NCAA Sports.

If you are currently in high school and considering attempting to play college golf, make sure you do the following:

- Talk to your guidance counselor and golf coach immediately. You and your coach or counselor will need to take several steps beginning with contacting the NCAA Initial-Eligibility Clearinghouse. You must include a registration fee of approximately $30.

- Make preliminary decisions about which colleges you are considering. The eligibility requirements for sports participation can differ depending on whether you select a Division I, II or III school.

- Work with your school counselor to determine if your current class schedule meets college admission and NCAA requirements. Prepare for and take the necessary college entrance exams (the SAT or the ACT). Study the NCAA eligibility guidelines carefully. Some requirements are extremely precise, including the fact that you must take your SAT or ACT test on a scheduled national test day. When it comes to maintaining your eligibility for a college scholarship, or even just participation at the college level, you get one chance to do it right, so as they say – don't blow it!

- Remember that specific rules apply if you are a home-schooled student or if you take correspondence or independent study courses.

- After you register with the Clearinghouse, you, your school coach, counselor, your parents, or an alumnus of the school need to let golf coaches know you are interested in attending their college.

College coaches may be interested in which amateur and junior golf events you will be playing in the future, so that someone from the college can observe your play. If you live far from the location of the college, the coach may wish to see a videotape of your swing. For more on videotaping golf swings see section 5.3.2, Your Swing Coach.

HINT: Unlike college recruiters for basketball and football, golf recruiters and coaches often do not attend high school golf competitions. Instead, they attend regional events where they have the opportunity to scout the best players from many schools. Examples of this type of event are an American Junior Golfer Association (AJGA) Tournament or a USGA Junior Golf Tournament.

The USGA website lists all requirements for maintaining amateur status. Visit **www.usga.org/rules/amateur_status_link.html**. They also welcome questions by email, mail, fax, or phone.

As you look at prospective colleges and universities, you should also think about your intended course of study. Many future professional players work toward a degree in business or marketing, anticipating developing their own line of golf equipment, a golf resort or a teaching program, or simply thinking they can be better prepared to manage the millions they plan to win. Others major in communications, planning that they may someday like to commentate for television sports.

A major in physical education is an option for those who consider coaching golf might be in their future. Depending on which college you attend, you might also earn a degree in sports psychology, sports medicine, or sports marketing.

Some colleges offer programs in turf management, and the related fields of agronomy. These programs prepare you to work as a Golf Course Superintendent; a career that you may not have realized can merit a six-figure salary. According to 1998 research from the Golf Course Superintendents of America Association, the average annual salary for this position is over $53,000. For additional information on careers as a Golf Course Superintendent, see section 4.5, Related Golf Careers.

PGA-PGM Degree

In conjunction with the PGA of America, select colleges offer a degree program called PGA/Professional Golf Management. A PGA-PGM degree prepares you to manage a golf course, work as a teaching professional, or take on other careers in the golf industry. Your degree may be in Marketing, Business, Hospitality Administration, or Park Management. When you complete the roughly four and a half year program, you have also completed much of the PGA of America's certification program as a Golf Professional (a club pro).

Along with other requirements you must meet, you must demonstrate a certified playing handicap of 8 or lower to enroll in a PGA/PGM program. Schools accept limited enrollments, typically around 300 per school program. If you are interested in this route, begin your application process early in the academic year for the fall semester in which you seek to enroll.

The following universities currently offer the PGA-PGM program, and the list is constantly growing.

Arizona State University East

> 7001 East Williams Field Road
> Building 20
> Mesa, Arizona 85212
> Phone: 480-727-1017
> Fax: 480-727-1961
> **www.east.asu.edu**

Campbell University

> PO Box 218
> Buies Creek, North Carolina 27506
> Phone: 910-893-1395 or 1-800-334-4111 Ext. 1395
> Fax: 910-893-1392
> **www.campbell.edu/business/pgm**

Clemson University

> 263 Lehotsky Hall
> Box 340701
> Clemson, South Carolina 340701
> Phone: 864-656-2230
> Fax: 864-656-2226
> **www.hehd.clemson.edu/PRTM/PGM/program.html**

Coastal Carolina University

> E. Craig Wall Champions. College of Business Administration
> P.O. Box 261954
> Conway, South Carolina, 29528
> Phone: 843-349-2647
> Fax: 843-349-2455
> **www.coastal.edu/business/golf.html**

University of Colorado, Colorado Springs

(program launches Fall Semester, 2003)
1420 Austin Bluff's Parkway
PO Box 7150
Colorado Springs, Colorado 80933
Phone: 719-262-3661
Fax: 719-262-3494
www.colorado.edu

Ferris State University

1506 Knollview Drive
Big Rapids, Michigan 49307
Phone: 231-591-2380
Fax: 231-591-2839
www.ferris.edu/htmls/colleges/business/pgm

Florida State University

Hospitality Department
University Center, Building B
One Champions Way, Suite 4100
Tallahassee, Florida 32306
Phone: 850-644-9494
Fax: 850-644-5565
www.cob.fsu.edu/ha/pgm/index.html

University of Idaho

1215 Nez Perce Drive
Moscow, Idaho 83844
Phone: 208-8857176
Fax: 208-885-0558
www.uidaho.edu/pgm/

Methodist College

5400 Ramsey Street
Fayetteville, North Carolina 28311
Phone: 910-630-7144
Fax: 910-630-7254
www.methodist.edu/pgm

Mississippi State University

P.O. Box 6217
Mississippi State, Mississippi 39762
Phone: 662-325-3161
Fax: 662-325-1779
www.msstate.edu/dept/pgm

New Mexico State University

P.O. Box 30001/Dept. PGM
Las Cruces, New Mexico 88003
Phone: 505-646-7686
Fax: 505-646-1467
http://cbae.nmsu.edu/~mktgwww/pgm/pgm.htm

North Carolina State University

Department of Parks, Recreation & Tourism Management
Campus Box 8004
NC State University
Raleigh, North Carolina 27695
Phone: 919-515-8792
Fax: 919-515-3687
http://natural-resources.ncsu.edu:8100/pgm

Penn State University

201 Mateer Building
University Park, Pennsylvania 16802
Phone: 814-863-8987 or 814-863-2624
Fax: 814-863-4257
www.psu.edu/bulletins/bluebook/major/r_p_m.htm

University of Nevada Las Vegas

William F. Harrah College of Hotel Administration
4505 Maryland Parkway
Box 456023
Las Vegas, Nevada 89154
Phone: 702-895-3865
www.unlv.edu/Colleges/Hotel/

For additional information, contact the PGA of America Education Department at 561-624-8400. The website for the PGA of America offers more information on the PGA-PGM degree program (as do the websites for each college or university). For more on the PGA of America see section 4.5.1.

> **HINT:** If your degree program does not already include it, consider enrolling in courses on public speaking and business writing as electives. Both skills are helpful in dealing with the media, fans, and sponsors as you play professionally.

Resources

The National Collegiate Athletic Association

700 W. Washington Street
P.O. Box 6222
Indianapolis, Indiana 46206-6222
www.ncaa.org
- 800-638-3731   informational hotline, with excellent prerecorded answers to commonly asked questions
- 800-638-3731   helpful phone numbers and information about ordering brochures
- 317-917-6222   administrative offices
- 317-917-6888   fax

Initial-Eligibility Clearinghouse

P.O. Box 4044
Iowa City, Iowa 52243-4044
- 319-337-1492   administrative offices
- 319-339-3003   automated phone system
- 800-638-3731   forms request line

Websites

AJGA
www.ajga.org

PGA of America (Readiness Orientation)
www.pgalinks.com/pro/index1.cfm.html

USGA website
www.usga.org/rules/amateur_status_link.html

2.4.3 Golf Schools

Another choice for continuing your education is to attend a golf school (some are classified as golf colleges) before moving on to professional play. These schools are privately run and may or may not be accredited. Also, they may teach only playing skills, or they may include a golf management program to prepare you to run a golf course or to provide golf instruction.

In considering private golf school programs, study their placement results. Knowing how many of their graduates successfully gain employment in the golf industry is a good way to evaluate the strength of their curriculum and teaching staff. Be sure to find out how much playing time is included in any golf school program you consider and if your golf course and range fees are included in your tuition.

Two top private programs for playing golf while learning about the golf industry are:

Professional Golfers Career College

27431 Enterprise Circle West
Temecula, California 92590
P.O. Box 892319
Temecula, California 92589 2319
Phone: 800-877-4380 or 909-693-2963
Fax: 909-693-2863
Email (Administration/Information): admin@progolfed.com
Email (Admissions): admissions@progolfed.com
www.progolfed.com

The Professional Golfers Career College (PGCC) offers a unique program for earning an occupational associate degree as a golf professional. PGCC's mission is that of educating its students to meet the golf industry's need for professionals who are trained in both the sport and its business management. It is recognized throughout the golf industry as a stepping-stone into the golf world.

The curriculum that provides students high quality education and instruction consists of four semesters over a 16-month period. Graduates receive a Specialized Associate Degree in Professional Golf Management. PGCC is nationally accredited by the Accrediting Council for Independent Colleges and Schools.

The dedicated staff is selected for their outstanding teaching ability and leadership in the golf industry. They include top PGA and LPGA golf instructors.

PGCC graduates become leaders in the golf world, occupying jobs such as club professionals, teaching professionals, general managers of country clubs, playing professionals, sales representatives of leading golf club companies and many other positions within the golf industry. The program has become well known and respected around the world with students from many different countries.

The program:

- Offers financial aid for those who qualify.
- Features a full-time career placement department.
- Has national college accreditation by ACICS.
- Awards graduates a Specialized Associate's Degree in Professional Golf Management.
- Is approved for Veterans.
- Provides instruction and play at championship golf courses.
- Is owned and operated by golf professionals.

San Diego Golf Academy

7373 N. Scottsdale Rd., Suite C-145
Scottsdale, Arizona 85253
Phone: 800-342-7342 or 480-905-9288
Fax: 480-905-8705
Email: sdga@sdgagolf.com
www.sdgagolf.com

The San Diego Golf Academy (SDGA) offers an accredited two-year occupational associate degree in golf instruction (preparing to teach golf) and golf business management. SDGA has campuses in San Diego, Orlando, Phoenix, and Myrtle Beach.

There are a number of other good schools that prepare you for playing only, and some that prepare you for playing and teaching golf. One of the best ways to learn where they are is to study their ads in popular golf magazines like *Golf*, *Golf Digest* and *Golf for Women*, then follow up by visiting their websites and requesting additional information.

You can find links to *Golf Magazine*'s Golf School survey and list of top 25 golf schools at: **www.golfonline.com/instruction/schools**.

Many of them will offer short-term instruction where you can attend for a few days without investing in an extended program. Remember, however, that none of this type of golf college or school competes in NCAA golf competitions, but while enrolled in their programs you can still compete in USGA and other amateur events, as long as you meet amateur guidelines.

2.4.4 Working with a Personal Coach

You may be one of the few who has natural talent that can be combined with a great deal of hard work, resulting in an outstanding golf game without formal golf instruction. Today's self-taught competitor is certainly aided in his study of playing techniques by the accessibility of televised tournaments, televised and online golf instruction, and the enormous number of books on playing techniques.

However, many people believe that structured training is essential for developing your game. For most players – it is. There are still a few self-taught players making it onto the professional tours, but even they, at some point in their careers usually seek instruction from a coach. (This coach is also known as an instructor. For more on the relationship of the established professional and his or her "swing coach," see section 5.3.2.) Golf instruction is available almost everywhere in the country. It is popular for even the occasional player to invest in a few lessons.

Since no two players approach the game in the same way, with the same swing, or playing style, no one instructional program works for everyone. Consider some of the factors that contribute to individual differences in play.

- Arm length

- Depth perception

- Endurance

- Fine motor control

- Flexibility

- Height

- Leg length

- Muscle mass

- Palm size

- Ratio of upper body to lower body strength

- Rhythm

- Spatial perception

- Strength

- Timing

- Weight

Choosing an Instructor

With this many variables in players, how do instructors decide what to teach? How do you know which one of those instructors to select? The decision is complicated and some pros prove this by changing coaches frequently. A few guidelines will help you in your game, and in selecting your coach:

- Start with good fundamentals. No matter how much swing styles vary from player to player, there are still fundamentals on which all instructors agree. Learn the basics and stay as close to them as you can throughout your professional career. True, some players succeed with unorthodox swings, but they do this in spite of their swings. Who knows how great they might be if they did not have to fight their swing style?

- Follow the established basics but do not push yourself into actions that feel unnatural to you. Each player personalizes the game with nuances that are unique to him. Do not try to fight what seems most natural to you, unless it is ineffective in play or conflicts with sound fundamentals.

- When you select a coach, pick someone whose advice works for you in tournament golf. Practice his or her techniques on the driving range, and then test the advice in tournament play. What may improve your swing on the practice range may not work on the golf course.

- Practice. Practice about twice as much as you think is necessary – or humanly possible. Concentrate during your practice and make sure you learn from each ball you hit. In the end, what goes right or wrong for you on the golf course will not be the responsibility of the caddie, the course designer, or your coach – it will be up to you.

Jimmy Falconer, a respected golf coach once explained the need to practice to a young player on a resort course in Florida this way:

"Sure you can stop practicing now, after all, it is hot today. But just remember, that somewhere out in a cornfield in Kansas is a young kid who is practicing his swing. He doesn't have the benefit of private instruction, like you do, or the opportunity to practice on a first-class driving range. But he is practicing. He's hitting balls into a field from daylight to dark. He's hitting no matter how hot or tired he is, or that when he has emptied his bucket he has to go and gather up all the balls himself to hit again. He just keeps practicing. You'll face him some day in a tournament and he will beat you."

Most one-on-one golf instruction programs offer individual lessons, half-day, multi-day and one week programs. They all offer the opportunity for the serious student to schedule a long-term training program customized to his or her needs.

Top Golf Instructors

Some top names in golf instruction include:

Jim McLean

Jim McLean is the 1994 PGA National Golf Teacher of the Year. He has worked with many professional players including Tom Kite, Brad Faxon, Liselotte Neumann, Len Mattiace, (two PGA Tour tournament victories in 2002), Christie Kerr (2002 Solheim Cup winner), and Jamie Vargas (#1 Junior in America, 2001).

McLean is a regular contributor to *Golf Digest* and the author of some of the best-selling books on golf instruction including *Golf Digest's Book of Drills*, *The Eight-Step Swing*, *The Wedge-Game Pocket Companion*, *The Power-Game Pocket Companion*, and *The Putter's Pocket Companion*. McLean contributed a special instructional section to the new book, *Hogan: The Man Behind The Mystique*. He is the Instruction Editor and Senior Advisor to The Golf Channel and appears regularly on The Golf Channel Academy.

There are two Jim McLean schools in Florida, one in Michigan, and four in California. The Jim McLean teaching program includes 46 world-class teaching professionals nationwide, all of whom have passed the rigorous Jim McLean Golf School training. CNN, *US News and World Report*, and *Travel and Leisure Magazine* rank Jim McLean Golf Schools the #1 golf school in America. Following are the Jim McLean Golf Schools. Contact them for information or visit **www.golfspan.com/ instructors/jmclean/jmclean.asp**.

Doral
4400 NW 87th Avenue
Miami, Florida 33178
Phone: 800-72-Doral or 305-591-6409
Fax: 305-599-2890

PGA West
56-150 PGA Blvd.,
La Quinta, California 92253
Phone: 760-564-7144
Fax: 760-771-2353

La Quinta Resort
50-200 Avenida Vista Bonita
La Quinta, California 92253
Phone: 760-777-4838
Fax: 760-564-7994

La Costa Resort
2100 Costa Del Mar Road
Carlsbad, California 92009
Phone: 760-438-9111 x 4258
Fax: 760-931-7552

Mariner's Point
2401 E. 3rd Avenue
Foster City, California 94404
Phone: 650-573-7888

Grand Traverse
4669 N. Village Drive
Williamsburg, Michigan 49690
Phone: 231-938-3775

Weston
2600 Country Club Way
Weston, Florida 33332
Phone: 954-384-4663

Jimmy Falconer

Jimmy Falconer, a member of the South African PGA for 38 years, is the former Head Pro at the Emfuleni Golf and Country Club (Republic of South Africa) and former Head Pro and Director of Golf at the prestigious Killarney Golf Club in Johannesburg, South Africa. Until establishing his own school, Falconer was most recently the Managing Director of the Phil Ritson Golf Institute at Orange County National in Orlando, Florida where Ritson rated him as one of the world's best teachers.

The Jimmy Falconer Golf School is in Florida. Falconer's students have included Ernie Els and Mizuno Open Champion, Eduardo Herrera.

Jimmy Falconer Golf School
2345 Fenton Avenue
Clermont, Florida 34711
Phone: 352-243-6910 or 407-492-0470
Fax: 352-243-6910
Email: NFalc75071@aol.com

David Glenz

In 2000, *Golf Digest* recognized David Glenz as one of the Top 50 Golf Teachers and in 1998, he was the PGA National Teacher of the Year. Glenz spent six years on the PGA Tour and is a six-time New Jersey PGA Player of the Year. He is the co-author of the instructional video, The 10 Fundamentals of the *Modern Golf Swing* and a new book, *Low Down from the Lesson Tee*. David Glenz Golf Schools are in New Jersey and Florida.

Glenz reminds players:

> "Coaching methods have improved over the years, and better coaching makes better players. Today's players have psychologists, trainers, and all sorts of resources to help them gain an edge. The important thing is to find a coach that can give you the time you need."

David Glenz Golf Academy
Phone: 888-SWINGFX or 973-209-6075
Fax: 973-209-1647
Email: glenzgolf@aol.com
www.davidglenz.com

David Leadbetter

Instructor to such Tour notables as Nick Price, Nick Faldo, Charles Howell III, Ty Tryon, and Se Ri Pak, David Leadbetter has been ranked as one of golf's top instructor's year after year. Leadbetter is the author of over eight books including *The Golf Swing*, *The Fundamentals of Hogan*, *Faults and Fixes* and *Positive Practice* as well as numerous top-selling instructional videotapes. He is a *Golf Digest* Teaching Professional and runs the David Leadbetter Golf Academy in Orlando, Florida.

David Leadbetter Golf Academy
Champions Gate
Phone: 888-633-LEAD(5323)
Email: info@davidleadbetter.com
www.davidleadbetter.com

Two Success Stories

There is no best plan that is right for every player. Two contrasting examples, straight from the headlines, are the young players Matt Kuchar and Ty Tryon. Both grew up playing golf, and happened to have opportunities to play at some top courses and work with excellent teachers. Kuchar finished high school, headed off to Georgia Tech to earn a degree in business administration and play college golf. He was not even considered the best player on his college team, at least not until he won the US Amateur the summer after his freshman year.

As the winner of the US Amateur, Kuchar received an invitation to play the following spring in the Masters. Despite a touch of the flu, he finished tied for 21st in the tournament. Runny nose or not, he was smiling. Matt Kuchar represented the perfect combination of youth, enthusiasm, and skill. The press and the fans loved him.

In order to retain his status as an amateur, Kuchar had to pass up his $40,000 winnings in prize money. Later that same year, he thoroughly convinced everyone that he had more than luck and a winning smile by finishing 14th in the US Open. Again, his $70,000 prize money stayed behind. And in case $110,000 was not enough to tempt a young man to drop out of college, Adidas, and other sports equipment companies offered him a few million more to turn pro on the spot and carry their bag or play their equipment.

But Matt liked – really liked – college. He passed up the endorsement deals and went back to final exams, frat parties, and NCAA golf. A few people thought he had made a wise move, but much of the media and the golf world could not stop criticizing young Kuchar for his decision.

Three years later in 2001, Tryon, the younger of the two, successfully competed for, and gained a spot in the PGA's Honda Classic. He began his opening round by shooting an impressive 67, and finished the tournament respectably tied for 39th. Tryon, only 16 years old, would have won slightly over $12,000. But as Kuchar had been, he was an amateur and claiming his prize would cost him his privilege to compete in future amateur events or to accept an NCAA scholarship.

Later that year, Tryon played again as an amateur by invitation in the PGA Tour's BC Open. This time he finished tied for 37th. While the prize money passed up at this smaller event was only $8,400, Tryon was beginning to decide that regularly declining such cash did not make much sense. With million dollar endorsement deals from Callaway Golf and Target as an enticement, the 17-year old decided to put college plans aside and turn pro. He did commit, however, to completing his final two years in high school.

Amazingly, a few people thought he had made a wise move, but much of the media and the golf world could not stop criticizing young Tryon for his decision. Was Kuchar, at 19, old enough and passing up the opportunity of a lifetime? Was Tryon, at 17, too young and unaware of what he was getting into? The message here is clear. No one else can make your career decisions for you. Do what you think is right for you.

The college grad and the high school student coincidentally turned professional within a few months of each other. Both seem happy with their decisions, although that first year on the Tour yielded less success for Tryon than for Kuchar, who chalked up two top-ten finishes in PGA tournament events, and early in his second season as a professional, claimed a victory at the Honda Classic. Tryon struggled with mononucleosis during much of his first season, and played few events and made even fewer cuts.

It seems the only thing that anyone can say with certainty about the decisions of Kuchar and Tryon is that both choices come with opportunities, sacrifices, and no guarantees.

2.4.5 Educating Yourself

No matter which career path you follow, you remain responsible for your own continuing education. The game changes. Better shafts, new club head designs, and balls that travel greater distance or with more accuracy hit the market each year. Advances in agronomy, construction techniques, and changing design trends produce different types of golf courses requiring different playing techniques.

One way you can continue your education is by reading the resources mentioned throughout this guide. Excellent instructional segments are offered at:

- The PGA Tour's Practice Tee
  www.pgatour.com/practicetee

- Golf Magazine's GOLFONLINE Instruction
  http://sportsillustrated.cnn.com/golfonline/instruction

- Golf Digest Interactive Swing Sequences
  www.golfdigest.com/instruction/swingsequences

- Golf for Women Instruction
  www.golfdigest.com/gfw/gfwinstruction

In addition to keeping your skills current, it is essential to keep up with the rules. Every year the governing bodies of the game fine-tune or completely rewrite certain official rules. The tours change their requirements for players. As a competitive player, it is up to you to stay current on all of the changes while at the same time pushing your game to keep pace with the competition. Playing skillful professional golf requires an education that must continue for a lifetime.

On the wall of the old Troon Golf Club in Scotland is a copy of The Golfer's Creed, written around the turn of the century by David Forgan, the son of a master club craftsman. An excerpt from the creed starts with the following line:

> "Golf is a science, a study of a lifetime, in which you can exhaust yourself, but never your subject. It is a contest, a duel, or a melee, calling for courage, skill, strategy, and self-control. It is a test of temper, a trial of honour, a revealer of character. It affords a chance to play the man and act the gentleman. . ."

Forgan's observation is as accurate today as it was when he first delivered the words in a speech at a Chicago Golf Club dinner, not long after his victory over Walter Egan in the very first Western Amateur Championship, played in 1899.

Know the Rules

Each player must assume responsibility to study and know the current year's edition of *The Rules of Golf* and *The Decisions on the Rules of Golf*. The USGA and The Royal and Ancient Golf Club of St. Andrews, Scotland establish and administer this rulebook and its companion rulings guide. (The USGA also publishes a video that demonstrates and defines many of the rules of the game.) Both are available online at **www.golfonline.com/rules** or **www.usga.org/rules/index.html**. They can also be found in most pro shops, or by calling the USGA at (800) 336-4446.

> **HINT:** Your $15 annual membership fee in the USGA includes a copy of *The Rules of Golf*, along with a subscription to the USGA publication, *Golf Journal*, and other goodies.

Test Your Knowledge

Below is one of the rules of golf that may cause players confusion and cost them penalty shots, if they make the wrong choices. See if you know the correct answers.

The rules of golf permit you to move without penalty certain loose impediments on the golf course. Which of the following are loose impediments that you cannot move during tournament play?

_____   twigs

_____   snow

_____   a fallen tree

_____   acorn

_____   ice that has fallen from a spectator's cup

_____   pebbles

Answers:

You may move twigs, no matter how large or small they are.

You may remove snow without penalty, but not frost.

You may move a fallen tree, provided it is completely detached from the tree stump.

You may move an acorn if it is loose on the ground. If it is mashed or embedded into the soil, you may not move it unless you are on the putting green. On the green, you may remove an acorn, even a partially embedded acorn. You may not re-pair any indentation the acorn may have left on the green, nor may you move the acorn even on the green if it is so deeply embedded that it is necessary to pry it from the soil in order to move it.

You may remove natural ice because it is a loose impediment. Ice that has fallen on the ground from a spectator's cup (manu-factured ice) is not a loose impediment; it is however, a mov-able obstruction from which a player may also obtain relief.

You may move pebbles, unless embedded in the ground, even if they are so large they are actually boulders, and it takes many people to move them. If they are so small they are sand, then you may remove them from the putting green only, but not from elsewhere on the course.

Confused? That's understandable. The official *Rules of Golf* are numerous, precise, and regularly revised or fine-tuned. The successful professional player has studied them in detail, makes the on-going study of them part of his or her regular routine, and knows whenever there is an uncertainty, he should call on a tournament rules official for a ruling before making a bad move. Thorough knowledge of the rules and how to make them work for you in competitive play, is an important skill to master.

2.5 Equipment and Clothing

2.5.1 Golf Clubs

The Right Clubs for You

Once you begin playing one of the major professional tours – especially if you are playing well – golf equipment manufacturers will want to meet you. During each tournament week, representatives from club manufacturers will be at the course practice areas with samples of their company's newest and best. They will have clubs, balls, and other products to give away.

They may also assign a clubmaker at their company to drop all his other projects and build custom crafted clubs to your specifications. Then, they will overnight ship this special order to the tournament site, hoping you will play their clubs that week. Many players sign lucrative contracts with equipment companies, and are well paid for the clubs and balls they play or the bag they carry.

Until you reach this level, you are responsible for supplying your own equipment. You do not need the most expensive clubs, and you can sometimes save money by buying used equipment, but you must have clubs that are right for you.

Custom Club Fitting

Check the sports section of your local newspaper, the bulletin boards in pro shops or ask a club pro or golf equipment retailer to advise you of upcoming "Demo Days." During a Demo Day, a custom clubfitter is at a golf course or driving range ready to answer your questions and give you the opportunity to hit with a variety of sample clubs. A club fitting session, available on Demo Days, assesses your swing, stance, and grip to give you clubs that best serve your playing strengths and weaknesses.

At some courses, you do not have to wait for a Demo Day because the teaching professional or a staff person in the pro shop is a trained clubfitter. In that case, custom fitting is available at any time, although an appointment may be required.

Many golf club manufacturers sponsor Demo Days. Adams Golf, Titleist, Ping, Ben Hogan, and Henry-Griffitts are some of the leaders in custom club fitting. Club fitting methods are classified as:

(a) dynamic, meaning they use information about the player's swing,

(b) static, they use the player's body measurements in the position of addressing the ball, or

(c) combination, using both static and dynamic information

Study golf retailers and equipment manufacturer's websites. The Titleist website at **www.titleist.com** offers an excellent flash video, while other equipment websites have information on schedules for Demo Days or on finding a clubfitter in your area.

The mastermind behind the design of Titleist wedges is club craftsman, Bob Vokey. If you own a Titleist lob, sand, or utility wedge, check it out. Look for Bob Vokey's name on your golf club. From his years of experience designing, building and fitting clubs for professional golfers, he offers this advice:

"When you gain membership on the PGA Tour, you will be surrounded by opportunities to play all sorts of equipment of every design. Remember the equipment that got you this far. Do not make radical changes. And, when you sign with a company to play their clubs, select a good company with the expertise to help guide you through the many choices that are out there. When you go out there to play, it is so important that you trust your equipment."

You can read more about Bob Vokey and Vokey Wedges at the Titleist Golf website listed above.

Fitting Session

Each manufacturer's methods of club fitting have similarities and differences, but the following account of an Adams Golf custom club fitting gives you an overall idea of what to expect in your fitting session.

1. The Interview Process

The clubfitter will first ask you questions about your game, goals, typical ball flight patterns, physical limitations, and other aspects of your play.

2. Determining Club Length

Based on static measurements the fitter will select a starting club length as a reference point. Proper club length translates to good posture, which is important to developing a sound, repeating golf swing.

3. Determining Club Flex

Based on a measurement of your club head speed, the clubfitter will select sample clubs. You will hit approximately three shots toward a target with each club, and then repeat the process. The fitter records ball flight information, including dispersion, shot shape, relative trajectory, carry distance, quality of contact, and your comments about the club. You will not know the specs of the clubs you are hitting – it is not about numbers, it is about proper fit. The fitter looks for consistent ball flight, without allowing you to hit so many shots that you adjust to the flex of the club (you would very quickly). The whole process is target oriented, like the game of golf.

4. Determining the Lie Angle

After determining correct length and flex, the next test will be for the proper lie angle. You will hit two-three balls off a shatterproof plastic lie board, hitting toward the same target you used before. A strip of electrical tape on the sole of the club will show wear marks where the club makes impact with the lie board. The position of these marks, relative to the center of the clubface, determines if (and how much) the club needs to be bent, either flatter or more upright to better center impact. This is key to improving distance and accuracy.

5. Grip Size

Grip size is based on measurements of your fingers and palms.

6. **Set Makeup**

The final part of the fitting is determining the set makeup (selection of clubs for your bag) that best serves your needs. You may already know which clubs you want, but be sure to consider the advice of the clubfitter. Carefully decide what you want your longest iron to be, as very few professional golfers use longer than a 3-iron in competitive play.

The total time in the Adams Golf clubfitting method is 20-25 minutes. It will be a relaxed and informative session. You will learn more about clubs and gain valuable insights on your swing. If you are uncertain of the meaning of any of the terms the clubfitter uses (such as loft or lie), this is a perfect opportunity for you to ask questions. There is rarely a charge for fitting sessions if you purchase clubs, though some manufacturers charge a small fee for the fitter's time if you do not make a purchase.

Which Clubs?

There is not "just one answer," as to the best clubs to make up your set. Seek the advice of more than one clubfitter; ask seasoned players and golf instructors. With experience playing different equipment, you will soon develop your own opinions. Moreover, as new equipment comes on the market and your own game develops, you will change your opinion, probably many times. But as a starting point, a generally accepted checklist of what you need to play competitively, includes:

_____ Your favorite driver and a back-up driver, because this is the one club your bag can never be without.

_____ A strong 3-wood (about 13 degrees loft) to sometimes use in place of your driver, to use on fairways where the grass supports your ball or to use in windy conditions.

_____ A medium 3-wood (about 15 degrees loft) to use on a course with fairways that are wet or in poor condition.

_____ A 4-wood (17 or 18 degrees) to use in medium rough.

_____ Your irons: 2-iron, 3-iron, 4-iron, 5-iron, 6-iron, 7-iron, 8-iron, 9-iron, and a pitching wedge to use on your approach shots and on many par 3 holes.

_____ Your wedges, including a 52-degree gap wedge, a 56-degree sand wedge and a 60-degree lob wedge for short approach shots, and pitch shots around the greens and from bunkers.

_____ Your putter. Most professional golfers travel with two or three putters and change them depending on the speed and texture of greens they are playing.

This adds up to 18 clubs, if you include only one putter. Remember, only 14 clubs can go in your bag during tournament play. Every year a few professional players are penalized or disqualified from a tournament because they inadvertently have over 14 clubs in their bag or because they have selected clubs and balls that do not fully comply with golf's official guidelines.

The Costs

Your golf clubs are the tools for your success. Do not try to save money by playing with ill-fitted or badly worn clubs; you will only impair the development of your own skills. How much you must initially invest will depend on the manufacturer you select and whether you purchase new or used equipment. The 18 suggested clubs would cost between $2,000 and $5,000, depending on just how prudently you shop.

Maintenance of Your Clubs

How long your clubs remain precision tools depends, in part, on how clean, dry, and rust-free you keep them. Even with loving care, a season spent in play and long hours of practice, especially in sandy soil, will wear the grooves on your clubfaces until they are no longer suitable for tournament competition. This does not necessarily mean your worn clubs must be trashed. A good club repair shop offers many services including frequency testing, adjustments of lofts and lies, re-gripping, re-shafting and even re-grooving of clubs to keep them at top performance.

Once you have selected your clubs, you need a roomy, sturdy golf bag with a strong comfortable shoulder strap. Consider the weight of the bag itself for times you may be acting as your own caddie. Every additional half-pound takes on new significance when you face the back nine on a hot summer day, endeavoring to put all your energy into your longest and most accurate drives.

Your drivers, 3-wood and 4-wood (also called metal-woods) need head covers. To protect the investment you make in your clubs, particularly if you and your clubs will be traveling by plane, you need a travel bag. Travel bags of molded plastic, canvas, or durable synthetics have room for your golf bag loaded with clubs. Travel bags come in different sizes. Some can hold only your bag and 14 clubs, while others easily hold 20 to 30 clubs and perhaps last week's dirty laundry!

Even if you are one of a tour's road warriors and travel exclusively by car, your bag and clubs will get considerable abuse on the back of a golf cart or in the trunk of a car. At the very least, protect your clubs with head covers.

> **HINT:** Read *What's In My Bag?* It is a peek into the golf bags of touring pros, profiling a different player each month. You can access this website from any of the following sites, under the heading, Equipment.
>
> *Golf Digest*
> **www.golfdigest.com**
>
> *Golf for Women*
> **www.golfforwomen.com**
>
> *Golf World*
> **www.golfworld.com**
>
> *Golf World Business*
> **www.golfworldbusiness.com**

You can also learn more by reading equipment catalogues such as Golfsmith at **www.golfsmith.com**.

Are You Really Ready to Play?

Here is a checklist of items other than your clubs, balls, gloves, and spare shoes that you will want in your golf bag on tournament day. Many of these items are available at tournament sites; but the selection offered may not include your brand or style of choice. (A printable copy of this checklist is included on the CD-ROM.)

____ Your favorite sunscreen; one that will not sting your face or cause your hands to transfer oils to your grips.

____ Your favorite tees. While extra tees are available at most professional tournaments, if you like the extra-long tees, be sure to bring them yourself.

____ Your beverage of choice. Even though drinks are available on the course, you may not be able to get your preference.

____ Your snack of choice. This may include fruit, energy bars, or other nibbles that recharge you while you play, without sending you on a sugar or caffeine roller coaster ride.

____ Spare socks, in case yours get wet.

____ Bandages; bring your favorite if you have a preference such as cloth, mesh, or a specific size or shape.

____ Medications: Aspirin, acetaminophen, or other painkiller of your preference along with your allergy prescription, nasal spray, or over-the-counter favorite. Eye drops can come in handy too, for battling too much sun, wind, or pollen.

____ Permanent ink, felt tip pens: The type of sturdy, small nib pens you probably already use to mark your golf balls are the perfect pens for signing your autograph on anything from event programs to cap bills to t-shirts.

___ Your rain gear: You need a waterproof jacket and pants for the unexpected.

___ Golf towels: Courtesy towels are often available, but you and your gear can get pretty muddy; you may need several. Be sure the ones you use are laundered once with soap, then once without, and never with fabric softener. You don't want any residual laundry products leaving your hands or grips with a slippery film.

2.5.2 Clothing

More About Head Covers

The importance of heads covers, by the way, is not just limited to your clubs. What you put on your head when on the golf course is extremely important. You need a cap with a visor or brim to protect you from sun and wind. Experiment during golf practice to learn which style of cap or hat stays comfortably in place and does not obscure your vision, while keeping the sun and perhaps your hair, out of your eyes.

A visor may be your solution, but remember it does not protect scalp, ears, and neck from heat or sunburn. Remember that you are looking for sun protection for a lifetime of potential cumulative sun damage. A hat with a brim is a solution to keep sun and rain off the back of your neck. Consider investing in a waterproof hat, of the style called a bucket hat. For cold weather, a warm cap, such as a sock cap, is essential.

It Is All in the Footwork

You must invest in well-fitting golf shoes, and own at least two pairs. More often than you would like, you will be treading water to play your ball. It is a good idea if one pair of your shoes is waterproof. Construction in golf shoes and the advancements in making them waterproof have reached levels of technology that would rival NASA. For example, FootJoy, one of the leaders in high quality golf apparel, offers a unique laser fitting system to fit golf shoes based on the analysis of 10,000 separate measurements of your foot.

The choice of metal or soft spikes increasingly becomes less of a decision as more golf courses mandate the use of soft spikes only. While soft spikes sacrifice some degree of traction, the up side is that they are not as heavy as metal.

Golf Apparel

Your wardrobe for tour playing needs to be durable clothing that does not show dirt easily. Select fabrics that will stand up to commercial laundries, which soon become your home away from home. Light-weight, thermal clothing and waterproof jackets, especially clothing suitable for layering, are important. Do not forget to include regular gloves for warming up your hands between shots on cold days and leather golf gloves for every time you play. And of course, that so-called 15th club in your bag, the golf umbrella.

Most players find a rain suit – a waterproof jacket or vest and pants worn over other clothing – essential. A common misconception is that rain halts tournament play. In fact, only threatening lightening, or water standing so deeply on the greens that it impedes play are sufficient to pull the players off the course. In PGA Tour events, the common practice to help keep players playing when heavy rains are expected, is to cut golf holes in the highest parts of the greens.

Dress Codes

For tournament play, or play and practice at most golf courses, men need slacks. Women may wear shorts, slacks or sports skirts. On some occasions or in some tournaments, men may wear shorts during tournament play. Always check tournament rules before you or your caddie show up flaunting bare legs.

Classic golf shirts, typically cottons with collars are the best choice. Do not wear images, statements, or distracting patterns on your golf apparel. Most golf courses mandate that you wear only collared shirts and no denim shirts or slacks, ever.

There are a few players, like Jesper Parnavik, who have successfully made quirky garments part of their image. It is a good idea to wait until you can play like this Ryder Cup team member and five-time PGA Tour winner before you decide to wear the brim of your hat turned upside down and sport attention-getting pink or purple plaid slacks. Just keep your look neat, pressed, and professional. Get attention with your game, not your attitude, or your attire.

2.5.3 Clothing and Equipment Contracts

Your worries about what to wear on tour end if you sign a clothing contract. You will have a new source of income, a new wardrobe, and the privilege of throwing away your dirty clothes. (Now that is one way to solve the headache of keeping up with your dirty laundry while on the road!)

When you are playing regularly on the PGA, Champions, or LPGA Tour, clothing manufacturers will approach you to wear their clothing line in tournament play. They will provide you a generous supply of shirts, slacks, or caps for the playing season and pay you a retainer for wearing them in tournaments. If you have the same caddie each week – especially if that caddie is well recognized by the public – the company may even include shirts and caps for him or her. Because they will want their garments to always appear at their best, they will ask you to never wear an item more than once. Many professional golfers either throw away or give away shirts after only one wearing.

One unusual twist in a clothing contract came for European Tour player, Vann Phillips. After signing a clothing endorsement with a leading manu-facturer of men's neckties, Phillips played all of his events that sea-son, wearing a dress shirt and tie.

Typically clothing contracts will be about $10,000 to $25,000 per year, but can go up to a $1 million, if you are a top name player. The contract includes built-in bonuses so that you receive extra payments for each win, or each top finish.

Equipment contracts regarding the clubs, balls and bags you play are generally more generous agreements than clothing contracts. They can pay retainers from $25,000 to $150,000, but sometimes run as high as $2 million for top players. Additionally, you can receive bonuses for wins and top finishes, with the highest bonuses paid for wins of Majors. If negotiating such payoffs strikes you as complex or stressful, you may find you would rather focus on golf and leave deal making to a sports agent. You can find information about agents in section 5.1.

2.6 The World of Professional Golf

As you venture into the world of professional golf, you need to quickly get a grasp of the structure behind the game – the organizations and their tournaments. As a professional golfer, you will be a self-employed businessperson. You cannot get away with only playing great golf (as if this is a small feat!). You must also understand who's who and what's what in the industry. This section helps you see golf in the big picture, with more details explained throughout the guide.

2.6.1 Golf Organizations

There are two types of golf organizations you will need to know about – associations and professional playing tours.

Associations

In the United States, amateur and professional golf is guided by the United States Golf Association (USGA) and The PGA of America. The Royal and Ancient Golf Club of St. Andrews, Scotland governs golf outside the U.S. and Canada.

Royal and Ancient Golf Club of St. Andrews

Golf traces its historic roots at least to the 1400's, and perhaps to even earlier in ancient Egypt, to a game played with sticks and round stones. In 1754, a small private society of golfers was established in Scotland under the name, The Royal and Ancient Golf Club of St. Andrews. This group developed over the years into the foremost authority on the game of golf.

The R&A today establishes the rules of golf worldwide for all play except in the US and Canada or in US professional tournaments conducted outside the US. They work with USGA on setting the rules and golf equipment standards, but there are some differences between the guidelines the two groups follow. Like the USGA, the R&A supports studies and research on golf as a business, conservation, and greens keeping techniques. Each year they conduct the Open Championship (the British Open).

To learn more about the history and traditions of the Royal and Ancient contact them directly or visit their website.

The Royal and Ancient Golf Club of St. Andrews
Fife, Scotland
KY 16 9JD
United Kingdom
Phone: +44 (0)1334 460000
Fax: +44 (0)1334 460001
www.randa.org

The United States Golf Association

The USGA improves the quality of playing experiences and expands playing opportunities in recreational, amateur, and professional golf.

In conjunction with The Royal & Ancient Golf Club, the USGA writes and interprets the Rules of Golf and produces the Rules of Amateur Status. They maintain the world-wide-accepted handicapping system for all players, and set standards for golf equipment testing to help preserve the balance between technology and talent. The USGA is actively involved in expanding golf education and golf opportunities, supporting turf grass research and assisting golf courses in evaluating their agronomical needs.

The USGA conducts the US Open, the US Women's Open, the US Senior Open, ten national amateur championships, and the State Team Championship. They help conduct the Walker Cup, the Curtis Cup matches and the Men's and Women's World Amateur Teams Championships.

You will find more detail about the USGA and its significant influence on the game throughout this guide. You can contact them directly or visit their website.

USGA
Liberty Corner Road
P.O. Box 708
Far Hills, New Jersey 07931
Phone: 908-234-2300
Fax: 908-234-9687
www.usga.org

The PGA of America

The PGA of America, based in Palm Beach Gardens, Florida, promotes the game of golf for all players. They focus on improving and standardizing golf instruction and expanding opportunities for play. The PGA of America provides certificated and degreed educational programs for becoming a golf instructor or for careers in the many aspects of the industry. Members of the PGA of America may play professionally, teach, or have other golf-related careers. Frequently PGA of America professionals have positions called club pros or golf pros.

As a professional player, you may choose to be a member of the USGA, the PGA of America, both, or neither. Each has different guidelines for membership. The PGA's are very detailed and include meeting performance and educational criteria. A membership in either organization has benefits but is not required in order to play professionally.

PGA of America
100 Avenue of Champions
Palm Beach Gardens, Florida 33418
Phone: 561-624-8400
Fax : 561-624-8448
www.pga.com

Canadian Professional Golfers' Association

Founded in 1911, the Canadian Professional Golfers' Association is the oldest professional golf association in North America. The CPGA represents over 3,000 professional golfers and golf pros across Canada. The association establishes the code of ethics and performance standards for the profession, and organizes the Canadian PGA Championship, the Women's Canadian PGA Championship, and the Canadian PGA Seniors Championship. Find more information about Canadian golf in section 4.2.3.

CPGA
13450 Dublin Lane
RR #1
Acton, Ontario, Canada L7J2W7
Phone: 519-853-5450
Fax: 519-853-5449
www.cpga.com

Tours

A tour is a business that conducts a schedule of golf tournaments for players who have either paid or played their way into membership on that tour. The leading tours in the US are the PGA Tour, which includes the Champions Tour and the Nationwide Tour, and the LPGA Tour, which includes the Futures Tour. What's more, there are dozens of smaller golf tours (called mini tours) for professional players. Chapter 3 provides more information about some of these professional golf tours. You will find information about many other tours and playing opportunities throughout the guide.

The PGA Tour

The PGA of America and the PGA Tour are not the same organization. Frequently you will hear people, particularly sports announcers, mix-up the two or speak of them as if they are one group.

The PGA Tour is not involved in amateur golf or in golf education. The Tour represents only playing professionals (sometimes described as touring pros). Think of the PGA Tour as the NFL or NBA of golf. Like their counterparts in other sports, the PGA Tour is the top of the ladder for a professional golfer (typically male) in the United States. The PGA Tour includes the Champions Tour and the Nationwide Tour.

Today's PGA Tour got its start in 1968, when the Tournament Players Division of the PGA of America separated from the rest of that organization. In the early 1970's, the new group officially became known as the PGA Tour. This expansion changed individual players into members of a professional organization with business specialists at the helm of overseeing the players' interests. The PGA Tour established the primary goals of providing playing opportunities for professional golfers, protecting the integrity of the game and expanding its visibility worldwide.

The timing was right. Professional golf in America had gone from ten pro players and one amateur who competed in the first U.S. Open in 1895, to the PGA Tournament Bureau organized in 1932, to a sport with booming post-war popularity in the 1950's. The charisma of the young players Arnold Palmer and Jack Nicklaus, a golf-loving President named Dwight Eisenhower, and the technology of television to share the game with millions, enhanced the growing interest in golf.

Since the 1930's, events sponsored by the PGA Tour and its forerunners have produced more than $700 million in charitable donations. In the 1980's the Tour expanded with the organization of the highly successful, Champions Tour, originally called the SR PGA Tour.

Through a series of changes, the Nationwide Tour (most recently known as the BUY.COM Tour) evolved into a competitive field of future stars and seasoned veterans all potentially just three tournament wins away from their spot on the PGA Tour.

The PGA Tour establishes the rules and regulations for player membership and tournament participation in PGA and Nationwide Tour events. But every US PGA or other US Tour event, in which you participate as an amateur or a professional, follows the rules of play established and administered by the United States Golf Association (USGA).

The LPGA

The Ladies Professional Golf Association (LPGA) is the association of top female professional golfers. The LPGA maintains a separate division for their members who are golf instructors. These instructors are not LPGA Tour playing professionals although they are golf pros or club pros, and have a type of membership in the LPGA.

The LPGA has an affiliated developmental tour called, The Futures Tour. This tour is for female players who have not yet reached the ranks of the LPGA but typically have LPGA Tour aspirations.

2.6.2 The Majors

Each tour hosts an annual series of golf tournaments. Outside companies or organizations seeking publicity and a vehicle for charitable fundraising, usually provide the funding and workers to run each event. The supporting entity is called the tournament sponsor.

In addition to sponsored tournaments, there are special tournaments each year. Organizations other than the tours conduct these special tournaments, but tour members play in these events along with certain invited players such as members of international tours or winners of amateur events.

These tournaments also have corporate sponsors, but the fame and tradition of the tournament itself usually gets top billing over the sponsor. The golf world calls such tournaments the Majors. Both the PGA and the LPGA recognize certain tournaments as their Majors.

For a professional golfer, winning a Major is an honor far greater than winning any other tournament in golf. Winning all four of the men's Majors at least once is a Grand Slam. Only Gene Sarazen, Ben Hogan, Jack Nicklaus, Gary Player, and Tiger Woods have accomplished a Grand Slam. Of these players, only Tiger Woods has won all of the events within one twelve-month period.

Over the years, the LPGA has changed which tournaments they recognize as their Majors. In some years they have conducted more Major tournaments than in others. The result has created LPGA Grand Slam winners with only two Majors won, some with only three majors won and others having won four Majors. A few players have the potential to win five Majors because five different tournaments have been recognized as Majors during that player's career.

The Four Men's Majors

The Masters

Augusta National, Inc., owner of the private golf club, Augusta National, located in Georgia, conducts The Masters. Legendary golfer Bobby Jones, along with golf enthusiast Cliff Roberts, founded the tournament. The Masters is the only Major played at the same golf course every year. Always held in April, the tournament is rich in golf history and unique traditions. From the hillsides of blossoming azaleas to the 61 magnolia trees that line the entry to the clubhouse, this event leaves players and fans feeling transported to a time of mint juleps and Southern mansions.

The US Open

The USGA conducts The US Open. The challenging courses selected for this event demand as much in strategy as in skill from the competitors. The US Open is scheduled annually in June at an outstanding golf course in the US.

The British Open

The British Open is the oldest of golf's Majors. An American golf fan will call this tournament "The British Open." A British fan will always simply call it "The Open." In Europe, despite there being many re-spected tournaments, none compares in history or prestige to The Open. Always played on a links course, this July tournament seems to make a habit of surprising players with unseasonable and unpredict-able winds and weather.

The PGA Championship

Played each year in August, the fourth major of the year is The PGA Championship. Conducted by the PGA of America, this tournament field includes top playing professionals and top club pros. The site varies each year, but it is always a top rated US golf course. While not considered Majors, the PGA of America also conducts the prestigious Ryder Cup Matches, the SR PGA Championship, and the PGA Grand Slam Championship.

The Players Championship

A tournament played each year at the TPC Sawgrass course in Ponte Vedra Beach, Florida is The Players Championship. TPC stands for Tournament Players Club, but is also said to mean The Player's Choice. While this spring tournament is not officially a major, it is such a favor-ite of the players, and its prize money is so generous, that it is often called the Unofficial Fifth Major. 2003 marked the 30th anniversary of the TPC Tournament.

The Ladies Majors

The Nabisco Championship

The Nabisco Championship (formerly called the Dinah Shore) is held in March at Mission Hills Country Club in Rancho Mirage, California. The tournament honors the contributions of Dinah Shore, who greatly expanded popular interest and corporate sponsorship participation in women's golf.

US Women's Open

Near the end of May or early June, the USGA hosts the US Women's Open. It is held at various premier courses around the US and is the longest running tournament in LPGA history.

McDonald's LPGA Championship

Sponsored by McDonalds, the McDonald's LPGA Championship is the second longest running tournament in LPGA history. In recent years this event is always held at the DuPont Country Club in Wilmington, Delaware.

Weetabix Women's British Open

Beginning in 2001, the Weetabix Women's British Open took status as the LPGA's fourth Major. It is a co-sponsored event of the LPGA and the Ladies European Tour.

Websites for the Majors

The British Open
www.opengolf.com

The Masters
www.masters.org

The McDonald's LPGA Championship
www.mcdslpgachampionship.com

The Nabisco Championship
www.nabiscochampionship.com

The PGA Championships
www.pga.com

The US Open
www.usopen.com

The US Women's Open
www.uswomensopen.com

The Weetabix Women's British Open
www.ladieseuropeantour.com

2.6.3 Staying Informed

With two primary organizations, five predominate US tours, dozens of mini tours, hundreds of tournaments and thousands of amateur and professional players, golf needs reliable communication resources.

The tours communicate to their members by mail, phone, and email. You may be a player in a tournament, or hoping to get in a tournament, but not a tour member. You will not be on the member mailing lists, but you can still stay up to date on events in golf. For starters, all of the main tours maintain great websites.

The PGA Tour's website includes pages for the Nationwide Tour and for the Champions Tour. The LPGA and the Futures Tour each have separate websites. All of the sites are excellent, filled with interesting updates on tournaments and players. For most tournaments, you can get real time hole-by-hole scoring for PGA, Champions, Nationwide, and LPGA Tour events. The sites include players' stats and biographies, along with detailed tournament information and many helpful links. Special features like players' diaries and online chats are good ways to get an inside glimpse into the life of a tour player.

> **HINT:**   Golf websites post much of their information temporarily or seasonally. When you find guidelines, addresses or forms that you need, save them to a permanent file or print them immediately.

The Golf Channel

The golf industry has a television network devoted entirely to the game of golf, something few sports can claim. The Golf Channel, headquartered in Orlando, Florida broadcasts golf 24-7. They cover tournaments in the US men's and women's tours, the Canadian Tour, and the European Tour, as well as instructional programming, specials on players and events, and regular newscasts on the business side of the game. Even the infomercials they air have helpful tips for training and playing.

This network is available from many cable providers, and in the US, on satellite through Direct TV and The Dish Network. In Canada, The Golf Channel is available through Star Choice and ExpressVu.

The Golf Channel also has a very good website, with hole-by-hole coverage of many events, programming information, news releases and on-line instruction. Visit **www.thegolfchannel.com**.

Golf Publications

There are a number of outstanding golf magazines or periodicals. Some also offer helpful and interesting websites. Use these publications to keep current on events in professional, amateur, and collegiate golf, as well as to benefit from the wealth of playing tips from pros and teaching pros. Visit the websites for the suggested periodicals listed below.

Golf Digest
www.golfdigest.com

Golf For Women
www.golfforwomen.com

Golf Magazine
www.golfonline.com

GolfWeek
www.golfweek.com

Golf World
www.golfworld.com

PGA Tour Partners
www.partnersclubonline.com

USGA – The Golf Journal
The Golf Journal is the official publication for members of the USGA. It is published nine times each year, and is included as part of your membership package when you join the USGA. Visit the USGA at **www.usga.org**.

3. Playing on the Major Tours

Golf commentator and former four-time European Tour Order of Merit winner, Peter Oosterhuis advises:

> "New players often change their games after they make it on tour, but golf is the same game whether you are playing on a mini tour, the Nationwide, or the PGA Tour. Remember it is still the same game."

As Peter Oosterhuis points out, golf can feel like a whole different game once you reach one of the bigger tours. This chapter will help you understand more of what it is like to play at the top professional level required on the top tours.

You will learn about the prize money, who gets to play in the tournaments (PGA Tour, Nationwide Tour, Champions Tour, LPGA Tour), and how beginners can break in by doing well at a National Qualifying Tournament (also known as "Q School"). You will also learn how to enter tournaments once you are eligible to play, and get insider tips for surviving tournament week.

3.1 The Money

3.1.1 Earnings on the Tours

Professional golf on the PGA Tour is a career path where average yearly earnings can most certainly mean millions. If you play in every tournament and survive every second-round field reduction (called the cut), yet you always finish in last place, you will still take home roughly $250,000 in prize money at the end of the year. Not a bad paycheck for being the guy (or girl) who comes in last.

Improve your position in some of those tournaments and you quickly move near the seven-figure salary range. Now endorse a few golf products and call yourself a millionaire. In fact, for many players, some years' earnings from endorsements surpass tournament winnings.

Realistically, the idea of playing in every tournament, making every cut and always finishing last, would be very unlikely. No career player, not even Tiger Woods, has made every cut in every tournament in which he or she has played. Nor does any player finish consistently last – or first for that matter.

And few players tee it up in every tournament. Travel logistics, and wear and tear on the mind and body make this difficult, though it is possible. Most professional players find that after three to four weeks of tournament competition, interrupted only by airports and hotels, they need at least a mental break if not physical rest. Other players skip tournaments because they wish to spend time with their families or perhaps need to work with their swing coach.

In addition, while golf is not a contact sport, the bodies of professional golfers know it can be taxing. With adrenaline flowing and players pounding the ball at club head speeds in excess of 120 miles per hour, joints feel the impact, whether the player realizes it at the time or not. Multiply the intensity of play by the repetition of practice, and you have a player hitting hundreds of high impact shots week after week, which quickly becomes year after year. No player escapes without damage to his or her body or the occasional need for medical attention and some down time.

3.1.2 Tournament Prize Money

The amount of prize money, called the tournament purse, varies in each tournament and from year to year. The purse is the combined amount of winnings by all players who receive prize money in one tournament. On the PGA Tour, (regular Tour events, not the Champions or Nationwide Tours) a single tournament purse may be as low as about $2 million or as high as $6 million, with about $3.5 million being the average purse.

The Tournament Player's Championship (a special event) has a purse of $6 million dollars, which translates to over $1 million paid to the winner and over $11,000 to the player who makes the cut and finishes in last place.

Distribution of the purse is based on percentages. No matter the purse size, the winner receives prize money equal to 18% of the total purse. All other prizes are also based on percentages of the total purse, but variables other than percentages alone determine the actual amount the player receives. Within each tournament, both the number of players to make the cut and the number of players who finish the tournament sharing the same score affect how much of the purse each player receives.

Every tournament has only one winner. A playoff determines the champion, in the event two or more players tie at the same low score after completion of all scheduled rounds. But playoffs only determine the winner. All other positions in a tournament can end in ties. In every tournament, several players will tie at the same scores.

If a tournament finishes like Example (1), shown below, then ten players would hold the top ten spots. Each of the ten players earns an established percentage of the total purse. For example, if this tournament has a purse of $3 million, the prize money is distributed as shown below.

Example (1) – Lowest scoring ten players

Position	Player's Name	1	2	3	4	Total	Prize $
1	Joe Golfer	63	65	62	66	256	$540,000
2	Jack Driver	64	66	63	64	257	$324,000
3	Bill Putter	65	64	66	64	259	$204,000
4	Frank Hole-in-One	66	66	63	65	260	$144,000
5	Dan Divot	66	66	65	66	263	$120,000
6	Max Sandtrap	66	66	67	66	265	$100,500
8	Frank Eagle	69	68	67	63	267	$ 93,000
9	Bo Wedgeplay	66	66	69	67	268	$ 87,000
10	Ted WaterHazard	67	67	66	70	270	$ 81,000

In a real tournament, scoring is never evenly distributed like shown in Example (1). Instead, many players will share the same final total score after four rounds of play. When this happens, several players share the same tournament positions.

Example (2) shown below, shows how a tournament's top ten can be more than ten players, top 20 more than 20 players, etc.

Example (2) – Lowest scoring eleven players

Position	Player's Name	1	2	3	4	Total	Prize $
1	Joe Golfer	63	65	62	66	256	$540,000
T2	Jack Driver	64	66	63	64	257	$224,000
T2	Bill Putter	65	64	63	64	257	$224,000
T2	Frank Hole-in-One	66	64	63	64	257	$224,000
T5	Dan Divot	66	66	65	66	263	$114,000
T5	Max Sandtrap	67	65	64	67	263	$114,000
7	Ben Birdie	66	65	67	66	265	$100,500
T8	Frank Eagle	69	68	67	63	267	$ 90,000
T8	Bo Wedgeplay	65	66	69	67	267	$ 90,000
T10	Ted WaterHazard	67	67	66	70	270	$ 78.000
T10	Chip Caddiemaster	66	66	69	69	270	$ 78,000

To distribute prize money fairly in the event of ties, the purse amounts are added together and divided by the number of players tied at one position.

Example: Jack, Bill, and Frank share 2nd place. No one is in 3rd or 4th places because the 3rd and 4th players tie in 2nd place. The prize money for 2nd plus 3rd plus 4th are then added together into a total amount. In this case, that amount equals $672,000. This total is divided by the number of players sharing the position (three in this example). Each of the three players tied for 2nd receives the new amount, which for Example (2), a $3 million event, is $224,000 per player.

3.2 Qualifying for the Men's Tours

3.2.1 PGA Tour

You do not have to be a member of the PGA Tour to play in a PGA Tour tournament. You can gain a spot in a limited number of tournaments as a temporary member of the Tour. If you are not a member of the Tour, but gain a playing spot in one of their tournaments, then you receive status as a temporary member of the Tour for that tournament week. But, you do have to be a regular member of the Tour to gain automatic eligibility into most PGA Tour tournaments.

With a few exceptions, the roster of PGA Tour members for each calendar year is set by mid-December of the previous year. Play and earnings during the golf season are the key factors in determining who plays in tournaments during the next season.

A look at the eligibility regulations for Tour membership and tournament participation quickly shows you that it is a complex formula. You, the player, are the person most responsible for following the guidelines and regulations of Tour membership, much of which involves meeting strictly enforced deadlines. As you read this section, be patient. It takes most players quite a while to learn and understand the system.

Fortunately, the PGA Tour relies on outstanding custom software designed to track players by rank and eligibility and on a staff of dedicated professionals.

Besides the players who are the past year's top money winners, membership on the PGA Tour includes players whose performance in specific tournaments, or over a number of years, has earned them their spot. While the guidelines vary slightly from year to year, the following describes generally, who is eligible to be a member of the PGA Tour.

> **NOTE:** On this list, the categories marked with ✓ are all avenues open to a rookie seeking first time membership on the PGA Tour.

Regular Membership

✓ The top 30 finishers from the PGA Tour Qualifying Tournament (for more information on Qualifying Tournaments see section 3.3) and all players who tied the score of the 30th player *(rule change from "top 35," effective with the 2004 playing season).*

✓ The top 20 finishers, based on official money won, in the previous year's Nationwide Tour official events *(rule change from "top 15," effective with the 2004 playing season).*

✓ The top 125 finishers, based on official money won in the previous year's PGA Tour official events. Tiger Woods, Justin Leonard, and Charles Howell III are players who gained their first year of PGA Tour membership this way, by receiving sponsors invitations to a few tournaments or Monday Qualifying and then winning enough money to place within that year's top 125.

✓ Winners, during the course of a PGA Tour season, of an amount of official money equal to the amount won in the preceding year by the 125th finisher on the official money list. This could gain you membership at any time during the playing season, as it is effective at the point your winnings equal the standard set at the end of the previous year.

• Any player who wins a PGA Tour cosponsored or approved tournament. This membership, too, is effective at any time during the playing season when a player achieves a tournament win.

Associate Regular Membership

The next 25 players who finish beyond 125th place in total tournament money won, in the previous year's PGA Tour's official events.

✓ Minor Medical Extension Members – Any previous member who qualifies for a Minor Medical Extension.

- Life Members – Any previous member with 15 or more years of active tournament participation, and who has also won 20 cosponsored or approved tournaments in his career.

- Past Champion Members – Any former winner of an official PGA Tournament.

- Other Categories include Special Temporary Members, Team Tournament Winners, Veteran Members, Temporary Members.

Now do the math. Add together just the categories of National Qualifying Tournament qualifiers (30+) and the top of the previous year's money list (125) and you have more than a full field for any tournament. While not all eligible players choose to play in every tournament, there are obviously still more members of the PGA Tour than there are spaces in an event. So how does the PGA Tour solve this?

The Tour gives first priority in tournament spots, called an exemption, to the winners of the PGA Championship, US Open, The Players Championship (TPC), the NEC World Series of Golf, The Masters Tournament, the British Open, The Tour Championship, and the World Golf Championship. In the past, this eligibility extended for a period of ten years, but after 1997, there was a change to giving five-year or three-year exemptions, depending on the tournament.

Exempt next on the list are winners of a PGA approved or cosponsored event. These players earn tournament eligibility for two years, which may increase up to five years if they win additional tournaments in a calendar year. Following the tournament winners are the members of the US Ryder Cup team and then the top 50 members on the PGA Tour Career Money list.

Other Categories

The following are other categories of tournament eligibility, not necessarily in order of exemption:

- Players returning from medical extensions.

- The top 30 and those tied with the score of the 30th player from the Qualifying Tournament *(rule change effective with the 2004 playing season)*.

- The top 125 on the previous year's PGA official money list.

- The top 20 on the previous year's Nationwide Tour official money list *(rule change effective with the 2004 playing season)*.

- Players invited by the tournament sponsor.

- Foreign players designated by the Commissioner of the PGA Tour.

- The PGA Club Professional Champion and other certain PGA section champions.

- Open Qualifiers.

- Previous winners of specific tournaments.

- PGA Tour Life Members

- The leading money winner from the previous year's Nationwide Tour.

- Players who have won three Nationwide Tour events in one year; this is an automatic "field promotion," permitting you to go immediately from membership in the Nationwide Tour to membership in the PGA Tour.

- The top ten players from the previous week's tournament, not otherwise exempt.

- Players who are Past Champions.

- Team Tournament Winners.

- Veteran members of the PGA Tour, which is defined as players who have made 150 cuts or more in PGA Tour official events.

- And a number of other infrequently used, special categories, defined by tour regulations, an explanation of which is available by contacting the PGA Tour.

When you consider that numerous players will qualify for a spot in a tournament based on more than one category, it is easy to understand why many PGA Tour members must pick up the phone, call the Tour headquarters and ask, "Am I in the tournament next week?"

3.2.2 Nationwide Tour
(formerly called the BUY.COM Tour)

For the Nationwide Tour, membership guidelines are slightly less complex. The following membership eligibility list shows that all eligibility categories are avenues open to a rookie seeking first time membership on the Nationwide Tour.

Membership on the Nationwide Tour

✓ Players who finish within the top 85 spots (and ties) in the annual Qualifying Tournament (see section 3.3). Remember, players who finish in the top 30 spots and ties, become members of the PGA Tour, but are still eligible to play in Nationwide Tour tournaments.

✓ Players who have won an official event on the Nationwide Tour in the previous year.

✓ Players who finish between 21st and 55th on the previous years Nationwide Tour official money list.

In addition to tournament spots for the members of the Nationwide Tour, there are 14 spots in each Nationwide tournament allotted to Monday Qualifiers, 25 spots allotted to the low scorers from the previous week's Nationwide tournament, and two spots, called Sponsors Exemptions, for players invited by the tournament sponsors. Most of the 25 low scorer's spots will not be used, because these players are likely to be already in the tournament through other categories of exemptions.

If, after including all of these players, there are still openings in a tournament field, then the list expands to include past winners on the PGA Tour, qualifiers higher than 85th from the Qualifying School and players who have won money in previous Nationwide tournaments during that year.

3.2.3 Champions Tour
(formerly known as the SR PGA Tour)

The Champions Tour boasts its own equally complicated criteria of membership and tournament participation. This tour is the PGA's professional tour for players 50 years of age and older, although the ruling on the age criteria is set by committee vote and could be either raised or lowered in the future.

> NOTE: On the membership eligibility list, the categories marked with ✓ are all avenues open to a rookie golfer seeking first time membership on the Champions Tour.

Regular Membership

- ✓ Top 50 players from the previous year's final Official Champions Tour money list.

- ✓ Top 16 finishers from the Champions Tour National Qualifying Tournament. *(This category is an on-going issue of debate within the Tour; look for the number of players gaining eligibility this way to be reduced after the 2003 playing season.)*

- ✓ Winners of an official Champions Tour sponsored tournament.

- Net top 70 players on the Official All Time money list. *(This category, too, is under consideration for revision.)*

- Players with special medical extensions.

- Members of the PGA Tour from the Past Champions category.

Associate Membership

- Current or former regular members of the PGA Tour and former regular members of the Champions Tour.

- Players who participate through Open Qualifying or Sponsor's Exemptions in a minimum of 12 Champions Tour cosponsored or approved tournaments during the current or preceding calendar year.

- Players who qualify for the final two rounds in the Champions Tour National Qualifying Tournament.

- Current Class A members of the PGA of America.

- Players who have won an official event on the PGA European Tour, the Japan PGA Tour, the Australasian Tour and the Southern African Tour.

- Past winners of the United States Amateur Championship and United States Senior Amateur Championship.

On the Champions Tour there are additional categories for Veteran Senior Members and players considered to be Super Seniors, meaning they are 60 years of age or older. Information on these categories is available through the Champions Tour.

Like the regular PGA Tour, the Champions Tour has more eligible players than the number of spots in each tournament, especially since the Champions Tour limits most tournament fields to roughly 81 or fewer players. To establish priority for a spot in a Champions tournament, the following criteria is applied:

Tournament Eligibility

- Top 31 players from the previous year's official money list.

- Top 31 players from the all-time Career Money List, provided they are among the top 70.

- Top 8 from the previous year's Champions Tour National Qualifying Tournament (this number may change from playing season to playing season).

- Players returning from special medical extensions.

- Qualifiers 9-16 from the previous year's Champions Tour National Qualifying Tournament (Q school) (this number may change from playing season to playing season).

- Players whose status changes because of a process known as the Reshuffle, that typically takes place approximately three quarters of the way through the playing season.

- Players with 70 or more All Time Victories.

- Winners of a Champions Tour tournament, who have a one-year special status.

- The top four players from the Monday Qualifier.

- Up to four players invited by the Tournament Sponsor.

- Past Champions who have won either a PGA Tour or a Champions Tour event.

- Veteran Senior Members of the Champions Tour.

- Super Seniors Division.

As detailed as these lists seem, they are only summaries of the very specific guidelines that the PGA Tour uses to maintain impartial and practical systems of tour memberships and tournament entries. When these guidelines seem to help your golf career, you will think they are fair. When these guidelines seem to hold you back, you may question them.

Keep in mind that these rules protect the interests of the players and the tournaments, not just for one event or one playing season, but for lifetime careers in professional golf. They were not established haphazardly. They began with a foundation of core principles and have been adapted carefully over the years to reflect the changes and growth in the industry. Most importantly, these are the guidelines, developed, updated, and approved by the players themselves.

3.3 National Qualifying Tournaments

To open the door to new players on the PGA and Nationwide Tours, the Tour conducts an annual Qualifying Tournament, also called Q School. More than a thousand golfers enter, but fewer than one hundred gain a spot on one of the two tours for the next playing season. Most of those who do qualify are players with previous tour experience. But in every Q School, a few talented rookies earn full membership on the most prestigious golf tours in the world.

The PGA Tour accurately describes Q School as the place,

> ". . . where dreams and opportunities meet. Where four-footers seem like different zip codes and tap-ins make your hands perspire."

Many players dislike the name "school," to describe these competitions. Qualifying Tournaments have little similarity to images of school days. They are in fact, some of the most grueling, competitive tournaments in professional golf. All players have the goal of avoiding return trips to the school, yet most professional golfers face it more than once in their careers.

3.3.1 Skipping School – Q School Exemptions

Every year the PGA Tour conducts the Q School in three stages. At the end of each season, players ranked as the top 125 players on that year's official money list, or who meet other tour membership requirements listed in section 3.2, do not have to attend Q School. Their place in most, if not all, of the next year's tournaments is guaranteed. Players not in the top 125 on the money list must return to Q School if they want to try to regain full playing status for the upcoming season.

All current year PGA Tour members are exempt from Stage I Qualifying. Other players (even those who may not be members of the Tour) are exempt from Stage I, or exempt from both I and II, based on their play and winnings in previous PGA Tour or Nationwide Tour events.

For example, winners of a Nationwide Tour event within the past five years (or its predecessor events, the TPS, Ben Hogan Tour, NIKE Tour or BUY.COM Tour) are also exempt from Stage I. Players who have earned a specified amount in official PGA Tour prize winnings are exempt from Stage I. A higher amount of earnings exempts other players from both Stages I and II.

A limited number of exemptions also go to certain foreign players and winners or top players in PGA of America events. There are ten exemption categories through which a player may skip Stage I tournaments and an additional five categories through which a player may skip both Stages I and II. The complete listing of exemption classifications is part of the Q School entry form.

3.3.2 Q School Requirements

The three stages of Q School are held in October and November, with the final stage sometimes held in December. If you plan to enter, the entry fee along with a completed entry form is due at the PGA Tour Headquarters by the official deadline, which is typically about September 15. Entry forms are available by contacting the Tour offices, or in a downloadable format at their website. You must send your application by US Mail or delivery service. Phone, email, and facsimile copies are not accepted.

> **HINT:** Follow all the guidelines exactly, as no concessions or special circumstances are ever considered.

There are no gender, education, or citizenship requirements for Q School entry, but the Tour has the option to reject any player based on conduct or other issues that relate to character. During tournament weeks you are not only accountable for your own behavior and dress, but also for that of your caddie. You face disqualification for inappropriate conduct, on or off the golf course, at any time.

Women may compete in the PGA Tour's National Qualifying Tournaments, but so far, it has never been attempted. Any woman competing would be required to play her ball from the same tee boxes in use by the men in the tournament.

Since the 2002 playing season, players attending Q School, are required to be 18 years of age by or before the last official tour event of the season for which they seek to qualify. If a 17-year-old player gains his playing card, he is a non-member of the Tour until his 18th birthday. He can play in some tournaments before his birthday, but is subject to all limitations and restrictions that the Tour applies to non-members.

If you have no tour status and have not competed in a Q School within the past five years, you must include with your application, proof of your scores and tournament rankings from two tournaments. These tournaments can be PGA of America Sectionals, mini tour events, or state, city, regional or metropolitan golf associations for amateurs.

Beginning with the 2002 Q School (held in the Fall, 2001) the USGA approved a change in its amateur-status code. Amateur players may participate in Q School. If the amateur does not receive tour membership on the PGA or Nationwide Tours during the school, he does not lose his status as an amateur player. Until this change, an amateur golfer had to choose between retaining his amateur status or participation in Q School, which could result in membership on a professional tour.

With your application you must also provide two letters of reference to your character and your playing abilities. At least one of these letters must be from a member of the PGA Tour or the Nationwide Tour. The other may be from a Class "A" PGA of America Professional and must include a copy of that professional's PGA of America membership card.

If you do not readily know professional players who might recommend you, and you plan to attend Q School, then begin networking in advance. In the early stages of your golf career you may have to approach others for help in the form of financial support, letters of recommendation or invitations to play in events. Learning to make contacts and present yourself positively and confidently is an important skill to develop as a professional golfer.

From your practice and play at golf courses in your area, you possibly already know several Class "A" professionals and maybe some tour players. Some of the players you have met in mini tour or amateur events in the past may now be current tour members. If you played on a college golf team, it is likely that you will know at least one player who turned pro sooner than you did and has already gained his playing card. If not, a high school or college coach, local club pro or your golf instructor may be able to help you make the contacts you need.

Make your call or send your written requests for recommendations several months before the entry deadline. Be sure to provide a self-addressed, stamped envelope for the response, as professional golfers have busy and usually hectic travel schedules. Submit the original letter with your application and keep a photocopy for your files.

Stage II Qualifier

There are six courses for Stage II qualifying. Because this occurs in November, only states with mild winter weather are included, again typically Florida, Texas, and California.

As in the first stage, the courses vary from year to year, and you may not be assigned to your first choice. Stage II reduces the final field from approximately 470 players to about 156. If you fail to make it in the first or second qualifying stage, you earn no money or status for your efforts – you gain only experience.

Final Stage Qualifier

Florida and California, alternately, are typically sites for Final Stage Q School, which may be scheduled as late in the year as December. The bad news is that the final stage of Q School requires six, stress filled eighteen-hole rounds. The good news is, you do not have to win to be a winner.

While only the lowest scorer gains the number one spot (and the best pay-off of the one million dollars plus prize money) the low thirty scorers all receive PGA Tour cards. This also includes all players tied with the score of the thirtieth player, no matter how many players that might be. Those players not receiving their PGA Tour card, but finishing higher than eightieth, all receive Nationwide Tour cards. The top five players earn prize money from approximately $50,000 to $27,500 each. All other PGA Tour qualifiers receive approximately $25,000 each and Nationwide Tour qualifiers about $4,000 each.

If you reach the Final Qualifier, expect to be competing with PGA Tour event champions and seasoned veterans. The competition is brutal. Players who fail to get their cards lose out on a spot in tournaments for the next season and will probably slide even further down the all-important money list of rankings.

Results of a single year's Q School affect careers the following season, and realistically, for a lifetime. And Q School does not get any kinder as players get older. The Champions Tour conducts Qualifying School and typically awards only eight playing cards with an additional eight as conditional – a number that may soon change to as few as four cards. Conditional cards mean that those players are Champions Tour members, but are only eligible to play in about half of the season's tournaments.

3.3.3 Fees and Expenses

Each player's entry fee is based on how many of the stages he is required to play. The full fee for all three stages is approximately $4,000, and may be increased in the future. Players participating in only Stage II and the final stage pay $3,500 and players participating in only the final stage pay $3,000. Players with no previous Tour status, must compete in Stages I, II, and III and pay $4,000. If a player pays the full fee of $4,000 or the two-stage fee of $3,500 and fails to make it to the final stage, he receives no reimbursement of his money.

Your Entry Fee Covers

- Entry into the tournaments at each stage

- Greens fees at the tournament

- Practice balls

- Shared use of a golf cart (for the caddie) during practice in all stages and during competitive rounds in the first two stages

Costs Not Covered

- Travel to and from tournament sites or at the site

- Accommodations

- Meals

- Caddie fees

- Other costs, such as equipment

A caddie during Stages I and II is optional but you are required to have a caddie during the final stage. Expenses to play three different tournament weeks, at three different sites, plus the entry fee itself, make Q School an expensive process. But, it can quickly become money well spent if you earn your PGA Tour card as a result.

Stage I is played at approximately 12 selected golf courses in the southern and western regions of the US. Most sites are in Florida, Texas, Arizona, and California, although there are always one or two options as far north as Tennessee or North Carolina. On your application, you must list your preference for a golf course, but there are no guarantees you will be assigned to the location you request.

HINT: Assignment to tournament sites for Stage I is on a first-come basis. If you play especially well at one of the sites, or it is convenient to your home, be sure you submit your entry on the earliest accepted date to increase the chances you will be assigned to that qualifying site.

Not all Stage I tournaments are scheduled for the same week, so the time between Stages I and II varies. Both stages are four-round formats with no cuts. At the end of Stage I, the twelve fields of 78 are reduced to fewer than 300 players. The exact number varies based on how many players are exempt from Stage I or II qualifying, and the number of spots that remain.

3.3.4 Champions Tour Qualifying School

The Champions Tour Qualifying School has two competitions or stages. The first includes six regional sites and fields of about 78 players at each site. Stage I plays four rounds, reducing the field after the fourth round to approximately the low 12 players per site.

These players, along with players exempt directly to Stage II, compete in a second four-round competition. The field is 108 players and only eight finish as fully exempt members of the Champions Tour; a number expected to soon change to only four. After the first 36 holes are played, the field is reduced to the top 70 players and those tied with the score of the 70th player. Golf language calls this a cut to seventy and ties.

The application process for the Champions Tour is the same as for the other men's tours, although forms are only available by contacting the Tour headquarters. Players must also prove that they are or will be, 50 years of age during the next playing season. Deadline for these November competitions is typically the first week in October. The entry fee is approximately $2,500 and those who have no tour playing history are required to provide letters of reference and information on their playing level, just like on the PGA Tour application.

3.3.5 Q School Can be Life-Changing

Sometimes players emerge from nowhere and gain their playing cards at PGA and Champions Q Schools. Most players try more than once to gain their cards. The current record for successful consecutive attempts stands at three years – no player has gained his playing card at the school for more than three years in a row. This is partly because a player playing at that level will probably finish above 125th on the money list and avoid having to return to Q School. It is also because Q School is unforgiving and the missed attempts and heartbreaks will always far outnumber the successes.

In case you still think Q School is not mind-boggling and life changing consider the story of professional golfer, Phil McGleno. Unfamiliar with his name? This is not surprising. McGleno went through Q School 17 unsuccessful times, before he decided that ole' Phil McGleno was never going to make it. In 1978, he had his name legally changed to

Phillip McClelland O'Grady. On his 18th attempt, now as Mac O'Grady, he gained his tour card. He went on to win the 1986 Greater Hartford Open and the 1987 Tournament of Champions. Q School is where dreams and opportunities meet – where lives are changed forever and sometimes even names.

Jaxon 's Q School Story

In 1999, rookie Jaxon Brigman finished the final stage of Q School with a total six round score of eight under par, after missing an easy six-foot putt for birdie. With great disappointment, he checked and signed his scorecard turned it in to the scorer's table, and started for the clubhouse to wait for the last players to complete their round. It appeared that the 35th spot – at that time the cut-off number for membership in the PGA Tour – would go to players shooting a total score of nine under par.

Jaxon, his parents and his fiancée watched solemnly, believing that Jaxon had played 14 rounds of great golf, only to now miss his place on the Tour by one shot.

But the courses at Miami's Doral Golf Resort are tricky and as the other players finished their rounds, numbers on the scoreboard crept higher. His family began to smile and other players started to congratulate him – eight under par was going to get in. Jaxon and any player tied with him, were soon to be regular members of the PGA Tour.

Jaxon celebrated. He would have a spot in almost every tournament played next year and he was about to put $25,000 in his pocket in the process. Then the unbelievable happened. A Rules Official came to Jaxon with Jaxon 's scorecard in hand.

He had signed his scorecard – an act taken very seriously in professional golf – and it showed an incorrect score for one hole. According to the rules of golf, signing a card with a score lower than a player actually shoots means automatic disqualification. But Jaxon had signed a score one stroke higher than he shot. He was not disqualified. He was however, required to accept the score he had attested to by his signature.

The one extra stroke took him out of 35th place and with a single mathematical error, off the PGA Tour.

Jaxon 's Q school story does not end here. While he lost his opportunity to play the 2000 PGA Tour season (by missing the 35th position), he was still eligible for membership in the BUY.COM Tour. Jaxon played the 2000 BUY.COM season and headed off to October Q School once again. He successfully completed the first stage, but finished the last round of Stage II, in a tie. Three players played off for two spots into the Final Stage of qualifying. His bogey on the first hole eliminated Jaxon.

In 2001, the PGA Tour changed the play-off rule for Q School. They now permit all players tied for the last open spot to advance to the next stage of qualifying. In the mind of one young golfer, this will always be thought of as the Jaxon Brigman Rule.

3.4 LPGA Tour

In the early 1940's, a small group of players organized the Women's Professional Golf Association. They funded it with their own money. With this shaky financial start, the WPGA folded after only a few years. Nevertheless, the idea that a women's professional golf organization was possible had been set in motion.

In 1950, the Ladies Professional Golf Association (LPGA) was officially established. Today the LPGA includes over 300 exempt and non-exempt playing professionals. They are the oldest and longest running organization in women's sports and the leading organization in women's professional golf.

An important part of the LPGA is the T&CP Division, or LPGA Teaching and Club Professional Division. Over one thousand female golf professionals belong to this division. They are teachers, golf professionals, facility managers, and coaches. The T&CP Division also administers programs for women and junior golfers as well as giving golf lessons to men, women, and children across the country.

3.4.1 Tournament Participation

Unlike the men's tours, exempt status on the LPGA Tour is determined at the beginning of each calendar year (or playing season) and is not immediately affected by mid-season tournament wins.

The Tour gives first priority in tournament spots, called an exemption, to players generally as follows, (remember the guidelines are revised annually and subject to change):

- The top 90 players on the official LPGA money list, through a specified tour event each year.

- The top 50 players each year on the official LPGA money list from two years previous, up through a specified tour event.

- The top 50 players each year on the official LPGA money list from one year previous, up through a specified tour event.

- Players with one career win within the preceding three calendar years.

- Players with two or more career wins, with the last win being within five calendar years.

- Winners of a LPGA Major within the past five years.

- Players ranked within the top 40 players on the previous year's LPGA career money list through a specified tour event each year.

- Players who gain their Membership at the previous year's Qualifying Tournament.

- Players returning from previous Medical Exemptions.

- Players qualifying through LPGA specified performance guidelines.

- The top five players from the previous year's Future's Tour official money list through a specified tournament.

- Players who are nonexempt but qualify based on past tournament wins (two spots only).

- International players who have forfeited their earned exemption.

- The next 35 players finishing higher than 90th on the previous year's official LPGA money list through a specified event each year, and are otherwise nonexempt.

- Other nonexempt tournament winners.

- Players who failed to gain membership at the Qualifying Tournament but ranked as the next 35 players in order of their results at the Qualifying Tournament.

- Other nonexempt players based on LPGA career money list and specified criteria.

- Class A or B LPGA Teaching and Club Professional Division members, eligible play one event per year.

The LPGA plays full field (144 players) events. For an open event the field will include 138 exempt players; two exempt spots for LPGA Tour Hall of Fame members and tournament winners with the most victories and career earnings ranking; two spots for tournament sponsor invitees, and two spots for players advancing through the qualifying round.

The qualifier round is open to LPGA nonexempt players and female amateurs with a 3.4 handicap or less and to Class A or B LPGA T&CP Division members.

3.4.2 LPGA National Qualifying Tournament

One route to getting membership on the LPGA Tour is to score well in the annual LPGA Qualifying Tournament. Conducted each fall, these tournament competitions are similar in format to the Q Schools on the men's PGA, Nationwide, and Champions Tours.

To participate in the LPGA Q School, you must meet the following requirements:

- Be either a professional player or, if an amateur, provide proof that you have an authenticated USGA handicap of three or less.

- Have been a female at birth.

- Submit an LPGA Application for entry and the processing fee to the LPGA office by the deadline. Currently the fee is $3,000 for one Qualifying Tournament or both Sectional Qualifying Tournaments. Only cash, certified checks, and money orders are accepted.

- Meet the eligibility requirements of the LPGA Constitution and be approved by the LPGA. Entries are subject to rejection at any time by the LPGA.

Entries should be made on LPGA forms, available at LPGA Headquarters, and mailed to:

LPGA Headquarters
100 International Golf Drive
Daytona Beach, Florida 32124-1092

For more information on LPGA Tour membership, contact the LPGA at 904-274-6200 and ask for Operations, or visit their website at **www.lpga.com**.

3.4.3 The Futures Golf Tour

The Futures Golf Tour is the official developmental tour of the LPGA, the largest international developmental tour, and the second largest women's golf tour. A developmental tour means just that – a competitive golf tour on which players develop their skills at tournament play while concurrently developing their skills as role models of the game.

With over 189 Futures alumni on the LPGA Tour, including Laura Davies, Tammie Green, Rosie Jones, Kelli Kuehne, Meg Mallon, Michelle McGann, Dottie Pepper, Grace Park, and Karrie Webb, to name a few, the Futures Tour is proven as an excellent place to play women's professional golf.

The Futures Tour conducts approximately 20 tournaments each year. Their tournament sites include locations in a dozen or more US states.

Purses average about $66,000 for each of the three or four-day events, all of which are full field tournaments of 144 US and international players.

The Futures Tour works to ensure that their events become valued parts of community life. Most of the touring players stay as guests in local homes during tournament weeks and devote time to ladies and junior golf programs at the event site. Since 1989, the Futures Tour has raised over $2.65 million dollars for charitable organizations.

Currently, after the Betty Puskar Futures Golf Classic each year, if you are one of the top five (updated for the 2004 playing season from top three) money winners on the Futures Tour, and you have played a minimum of six Futures events that season, you are automatically eligible for membership on the LPGA Tour for the following year.

Except for invitational events, most tournaments on the Futures Tour are open to:

- Futures Tour Members, in order by their ranked status.

- LPGA Tour Members (playing with permission of the LPGA).

- Other professional and amateur golfers who meet specific criteria.

Eligibility rules are complex and change slightly each season. You must contact the Future's Tour Headquarters for the complete and most current requirements. Do not hesitate to pick up the phone and call or submit your questions by email. The Tour staff is accustomed to explaining the ins and outs of requirements and eligibility, and will be happy to help you.

For more information on the Futures Tour, contact them at their Headquarters in Lakeland, Florida, or visit their website.

The Futures Tour
The Club at Eaglebrooke
1300 Eaglebrooke Boulevard
Lakeland, Florida 33813
Telephone: 863-709-9100
Fax: 863-709-9200
www.futurestour.com

3.5 Life on the Tour

PGA Tour member Brendan Pappas had five top-ten tournament finishes on the 2001 Nationwide Tour (BUY.COM Tour). He followed that great season by making the cut 6 times in PGA Tour events in 2002, then topping off his playing season by finishing T8 at the PGA Qualifying School for the 2003 season. He says this of life on the Tour:

> "I was surprised as I began playing professional golf, just how much it is like a job. It is not about a flamboyant lifestyle. It is about attention to the small things, like waking up at the same time each morning, eating healthy, and being so dedicated in your thoughts that you are willing to miss things in your life because you are following the dream."

3.5.1 Tournament Week

Golf fans who view televised tournaments only on weekends, sometimes forget that players are working throughout the week. For professional golfers on the PGA, Champions, Nationwide, or LPGA Tours, tournament weeks begin on Monday.

If you are a player already in the tournament field, Monday may be your travel day. Whether you will drive or fly commercially or by private jet effects which day you select for traveling. Also, if you have played and made the cut in the previous tournament you will still be competing on Sunday afternoon at another location, often on the other side of the country, sometimes on the other side of the world. Back-to-back tournament play clearly has both advantages and disadvantages for professional players.

For the players who are able to arrive early at the tournament, Monday is the best day to get in a good round of practice on the tournament golf course, without the distraction of fans, autograph seekers, or the press. Players sometimes joke and say that early in the playing season everyone gets to a tournament on Monday morning, but by the end of the season, many players do not drag in until Tuesday night.

Tuesday can also be a travel day, especially on the Champions Tour, where most tournaments are only three-round competitions instead of four. On all of the major tours, some players conduct clinics for Junior golfers or club members, or perform in exhibitions and shoot-out competitions at the tournament course on either Monday or Tuesday of tournament week.

Players normally do this without receiving payment. It is considered a way to give back to the sponsor who helps underwrite the costs of the event and it is a way to support the charities that benefit from the tournament. Of course, all players are always trying to play practice rounds on the course and spend plenty of time on the driving range. As a tournament competitor, you have to find a balance between the commitments of tournament week and the whole purpose of being there – which is playing your very best competitive golf!

There are one, two or occasionally three days before the start of tournament play when the players participate in ProAm (Professional-Amateur) tournaments. Amateur players of all skill levels pay fees for the privilege of playing a round with the professional players. The sponsor may invite television, news, or sports personalities to play in the ProAm as another way to attract amateur participants. ProAm days may include luncheons, cocktail parties or perhaps a brunch. They include contests and smaller competitions within the round of golf. ProAm events are very important to the tours because of the money, community interest, and goodwill they generate.

3.5.2 Player Perks

Each tournament varies, but typically, the participating players receive gifts and complimentary services like barbers on site, dry cleaning service, or other day-to-day conveniences they might otherwise have trouble fitting into their schedules. Players may also receive gifts that represent specialties of the geographic region where the tournament is conducted or products produced by a corporate sponsor.

Unrestricted use of a car and driver or the personal use of a car is usually provided to players on the PGA, Champions, and LPGA Tours. Players on the Nationwide Tour receive only complimentary transportation between the airport, hotel, and golf course.

A limited number of players stay as guests in private homes volunteered by local club members at the tournament course site. Most players prefer to retreat to a hotel room or rent full use of a private home. Players pay this expense personally.

A few players choose travel in custom vehicles. For example, one member of the Champions Tour purchased a motor coach outfitted with made-to-order wine coolers and all of his special requests. The finished motor home carried a price tag of over three million dollars – but if the comforts of home help him earn a few tournament titles, then this investment (already tax deductible) is a justifiable expenditure.

Because many players today travel with their families, the tours provide, either free or for a reasonable fee, high quality on-site childcare at each tournament. Some players choose home schooling or correspondence courses for their children for all or part of the year to make it even easier for their families to travel with them.

On the LPGA Tour, a fulltime childcare staff travels to each tournament in a mobile daycare center. Tour children find that their school's location may change from week to week, but their classmates and classroom materials remain the same at each new site.

Personnel from the Tour and the tournament sponsor assist players and their families at each tournament. A support staff makes sure that emergency and routine medical care is available if needed, helps with travel reservations, or may simply offer directions to the nearest shopping mall.

Many tournament committees also plan activities designed to appeal to the players, especially to their families. Tournaments want to encourage players to return year after year and play in the event. An example of planned activities might include fishing outings, hot air ballooning, or trips for player's children to theme parks.

The player's lounge area at each tournament is restricted to players and their immediate families. The lounge area, typically a section of the clubhouse, offers an oasis for players to retreat for privacy from the press and the fans. Buffet food service and short order chefs are often available, along with toll free telephone lines, data ports, and fax services.

Another valuable service provided for players is the equipment trailers set up by various club and golf equipment manufacturers. Skilled clubmakers, masters of their craft, staff these trailers. They patiently work with the players; building, adjusting, and refurbishing clubs to suit the player's week-to-week needs.

Many tournaments offer health care trailers with trained physical therapists, masseurs, and sports trainers for the players. To learn more about these services, read about the HealthSouth Fitness Trailer in Section 5.3.3

3.5.3 Tournament Staff

It is helpful to you as a player to understand the overall workings of a tournament. Planning and operating a successful week of golf tournament activities is hard work and involves many people. The National Golf Foundation (NGF) is the organization that provides certifiable record keeping and fact-finding for all business aspects of recreational, amateur and professional golf trends.

The NGF estimates that there are over 35,000 tournament events held each year in the United States – or an average of 96 tournaments per day, every day. While these are not all events at the professional level, this statistic shows the importance of tournament golf as a business. Tournament management is a business that succeeds only when players, tours, and sponsors work together.

Management positions for a tournament sponsor include the Tournament Director and any of the paid administrative, sales, marketing, and operations staff who report to the Director. The Tournament Director ultimately bears all responsibility for a tournament's success.

A tour will have employees in similar positions to the jobs of the tournament sponsor staff and the two teams work together. The tournament sponsor staff focuses on their specific event while the Tour staff oversees all of the events in which their players participate. The Tour will also have one or more positions responsible for developing new tournament and sponsorship opportunities. They are the Tournament Development Coordinators.

Along with the paid workers, each tournament will have a huge staff of volunteers who participate in return for tournament passes, the experience of being part of a professional event, and a chance for close contact with the players. Tours look for a sponsor to enlist a minimum of 500 volunteers, with some events needing as many as 1500 non-paid workers contributing to the tournament's success.

Behind every tournament there is a workforce of many exhausted people coordinating everything from crowd control to the port-a-potties to the caddie shack. One of the more unusual tasks a volunteer might be assigned is that of coordinating with the golf course staff to dye the water hazards. A temporary, non-toxic blue dye assures that golf course lakes look their sparkling best for the television cameras.

Some of the many volunteer jobs it takes behind the scenes to make a successful golf tournament include:

- **Caddie Staff** to oversee the registration of the player's caddies and to assist as needed.

- **Cart Staff** to assist the golf course personnel in inventorying and distributing tournament golf carts, and to taxi players, media or officials when needed on the course. They may also be responsible to transport handicapped spectators from parking to viewing areas.

- **Cash Office Staff** to assist the Tour and the sponsor in counting and reconciling receipts and in preparing cash banks.

- **Course Staff** to assist golf course personnel in staffing and maintaining control in the practice areas, the staking and roping of the courses in gallery areas, and sometimes the set-up and take-down of temporary structures like bleacher seating, tents, or television camera staging areas.

- **First Aid Staff** to provide emergency medical care during the tournament week to players, workers, and fans.

- **Food and Beverage Service Staff** to provide water, fruit, and appropriate snacks to the players, to other work committees of the tournament, and at key locations like the Scorers Tent.

- **Marshalls** to control and communicate to the gallery during play.

- **Media and Public Relations Staff** to promote ticket sales, publicity, and sponsorship opportunities, and to provide for the hospitality and needs of the press, the sponsors, and the corporate hospitality areas.

- **Measurements and Scoring Staff** to measure shot distance, ball positions, and putting distances with laser instruments, to walk with each group of players and record scores, maintain scoring records, assist on PGA Tour events with scoring or to serve as Standard Bearers, who walk with a group of players displaying scores for that group.

- **Parking Staff**

- **ProAm Coordinators** to register amateurs, assemble and distribute gift packs, schedule play, arrange complimentary guest photography, and provide scoring during ProAm events, (this becomes a tournament within a tournament).

- **Security Staff**

- **Ticket Sales** additional to selling admissions tickets, this may include checking of credentials and passes, management of Will Call advanced ticket sales, and maintaining a site like a Coat Check, for cell phones and cameras that spectators attempt to bring onto the course.

- **Transportation Staff** to coordinate the loan of automobiles from dealerships, maintenance, assignment to players and all courtesy transportation of players and VIP guests during and after the event.

- **Uniforms Staff** to fit, distribute, and supervise all uniform apparel worn by staff.

- **Volunteer Services Staff** which may include recruiting volunteers, maintaining databases, shuttling them to and from off site parking, scheduling, and maintaining a volunteer tent as a designated break and snack location.

HINT: Volunteering to be part of a tournament staff is not only an excellent way to learn more about the events of tournament week, but may provide you the chance to observe the Pros in play or practice. Visit the website for each tournament or call the host golf course to learn how to sign-up as a tournament volunteer.

Tournament Directors are always under scrutiny that each year's event is operationally and financially successful. The week has to be smooth running and pleasant to entice top-notch players year after year. Equally important to players is that the tournament offers a golf course in tip-top condition. The more notable players a tournament attracts, the more press coverage the event receives. This translates to larger galleries and more participation by additional corporate sponsors, which in the end, is what makes the tournament come out on top.

It is important as a professional golfer that you understand and value the efforts of the many people who help make professional golf events possible. When the tournament or one of its sponsors invites you to social functions to meet their employees or guests, try to work it into your schedule. Despite your skills and golfing talent, you would not have the opportunity to play for such high stakes, and charities would not receive such worthwhile benefits, if it were not for the sponsors and volunteers who make golf tournaments run. Sponsors, tours, volunteers, players, and fans each play an important role in the success of every golf tournament.

3.5.4 Entering Tournaments

As a player, if you are eligible for a tournament and wish to play, you must make a phone call to the PGA or LPGA Tour Headquarters' Player Commitment Line before close of business on Friday of the week before the event. This call commits you to play in the tournament, but does not register you.

Players on the Nationwide, Champions, and LPGA Tours pay an entry fee per tournament of approximately $100 and complete a registration form. Players on the PGA Tour pay no fee. You may submit your registration form and payment (if applicable) at the tournament site, any time before the tournament. You cannot commence practice until you register.

Players in a tournament sometimes withdraw from the field, generally because of medical or personal reasons. When they do, the next player on the alternate list moves into the playing field. If a player withdraws after he or she begins play, no alternate is added. The tournament then plays with a short field. Players who are high on the alternate list often travel to tournament sites, hoping to get in if another player pulls out.

Some players write to tournament sponsors and ask to be invited to play in tournaments. Each tournament typically issues from two to four of what the players call 'invites'. In his note or letter, most often handwritten, a player explains why his participation would be an asset to the field of the tournament.

Sponsors are, in general, already quite aware of which non-exempt players would be a drawing card for bringing the public and the press to the tournament and consider this as they issue their invitations. A sponsor's invite may be issued months before a tournament or not given until tournament week.

Monday Qualifiers

If you are a player not already in the tournament, you can gain a tournament spot by playing in the Monday Qualifier. Each week a few players play their way into tournaments in the Monday Qualifiers, also called Open Qualifiers.

Players vying for one of the limited spots as a Qualifier, compete at a course near the tournament in a one-round competition. The PGA of America local Section conducts qualifier competitions for the tours. In most PGA Tour events, there are four or fewer open qualifying spots per tournament, 14 on the Nationwide Tour, two on the LPGA Tour and four or fewer on the Champions Tour. Players sometimes call this competition, "4-spotting" for obvious reasons.

Tournaments that accept Monday Qualifiers may indicate this by using the word "Open" as part of their official name, for example, the Hartford Open or the Buick Open. All Nationwide Tour tournaments, except their championship events are open to qualifiers.

The fee to Monday Qualify ranges from $100 to $400, per tournament. In most cases, it must be in the hands of the Qualifying Tournament Staff, along with a completed registration form, by Friday before the tournament week. These entry forms are available through the tour headquarters or from the staff at the tournament course. A complete listing of Monday Qualifying sites and contacts for the men's tours is available at the PGA Tour website or by contacting their headquarters. Qualifying information for the LPGA is available only by contacting their headquarters.

For the Champions Tour, a player must be 50 years of age or older and must be a professional. On all of the other major tours, there is currently no minimum age requirement for Monday Qualifiers and they are open to amateurs. To be eligible to compete in a Qualifier, if you have no professional playing history, you must meet a handicap minimum. The requirement is a handicap rating of 2 or less for the PGA Tour and Nationwide Tour and 3.4 for the LPGA Tour.

> **HINT:** Unsure of your handicap? While only rated golf courses and golf associations that follow the USGA Handicap System issue an official handicap, you can unofficially figure your own, for your personal information. Study the USGA's webpages on handicapping so that you understand how the system works. Next, visit websites on handicapping and look into helpful downloadable software for estimating and monitoring your handicap rating.

After you turn pro and play once professionally, you will no longer be required to prove your handicap rating. You also have the option to play and accept no prize money, if you choose to maintain amateur status. The following websites have helpful handicapping information:

Official Golf Handicapping Site of the USGA
www.usga.org/handicap

Golf 101 – Handicap Calculator
www.golf101.com/Pages/Apps/Calculator/Calculator.asp

Scorekeeper Software by Mark II Systems
Downloadable sample; software available to purchase online, along with other golf software packages.
www.scorekeeper.com

3.5.5 Tournament Formats

Most PGA and Nationwide Tour tournaments play four 18-hole rounds, one on each of four consecutive days. Tournament days typically are Thursday, Friday, Saturday, and Sunday.

Both tours allow fields of 156 players with the Tournament Director having the right to reduce the field to as few as 144 players. Under special circumstances, the field can be more than 156 or fewer than 144.

A threesome of players can play one round of golf on the average golf course in approximately four hours and 20 minutes. A golf course with a large geographic area, or certain terrain features, may take longer to play. While the USGA Official Rules of Golf governs pace of play, playing time can vary depending on whether players are playing quickly or are using the maximum allowed time to complete play.

Because of a course's design, size, or the number of daylight hours (based on location and season) some tournament sites cannot handle more than 144 players in one day of tournament play. In most cases, the annual spring forward to Daylight Savings Time increases all fields to 156 players and reduces them again to 144 with the fall back to regular time.

Players may be assigned to play in groups of two or three players. It is most common that in the first two rounds of play, each group consists of three players. The final two rounds may be played with only groups of three, or only groups of two. The grouping of players and their assignment to a tee time is called the draw. The players you are drawn to play with in the first round will also be your grouping for the second round.

The draw is not a random process. It follows detailed guidelines prepared and administered by the PGA Tour. On the Champions Tour, the draw usually only applies to the first round of play. For the second and third rounds, players are drawn with other players of similar scores.

If you have an early morning tee time for the first round, you will have an afternoon tee time for the second round. Players speak of this as playing, "early-late," or "late-early." Players grouped in threesomes tee off in schedules of one grouping approximately every nine to ten minutes.

In a field of 144 players playing in threesomes, a tournament has a total of 48 groups. There are typically not enough hours of daylight to permit scheduling 48 groups to all tee off from the first hole on a golf course and complete their round before twilight. To solve this, the tournament splits the field into two sets of 24 groups. Twenty-four groups of players tee off (one group every nine to ten minutes) from the first hole. They play the course in sequential order, holes 1-18. The other 24 groups tee off (one group every nine to ten minutes) from the 10th hole. They play the course holes 10-18, then holes 1-9. If you start play on the first hole in round one, you will start play on hole 10 in the second round.

After two rounds of play are completed, the field is reduced. On the PGA Tour, the reduction, called the cut, typically is made to the 70 players with the lowest scores after the first 36 holes (two rounds) of play. Players tied with the score of the 70th player are included. Players who do not make the cut, do not play in the final two rounds. They receive no prize money. The number of players to which a field cuts will vary depending on the rules of the particular tournament.

Following the two round cut, a new draw is made to determine player groupings for Round 3. Players' scores determine the draw. Players are grouped with other players who have the same or nearly the same scores as their own.

If your score is high, expect one of the earliest tee times of the day, while if your score is low, expect one of the latest tee times. In general, this places the lowest scoring players on the course on Saturday and Sunday afternoons – the time when spectator crowds are the largest and television coverage is scheduled.

Nationwide Tour and Champions Tour tournaments follow similar formats to that of the PGA Tour for making the draw and grouping players. Nationwide Tour events are four-rounds of play with a cut, but Champions Tour tournaments are generally three rounds of play with no cut. The field in most Champions events, because there is no cut, is usually limited to approximately 78 players.

Champions Tour players are the only players permitted to use a golf cart during play at most events. Their cart use is restricted and only a player or his caddie may be in the cart, but not both of them at the same time. Cart rules, like many other tournament specifics may vary with each tour and at each event. Check the rules established for every tournament in which you play. You receive these guidelines as a handout at player registration, or they might be posted in the player's locker room and lounge.

The more you play in professional tournaments, the more familiar you become with the rules and the protocol for tournaments. Most rookie PGA Tour players find the PGA Tour staff helpful and always willing to answer questions. Also, there are mandatory training sessions for new players who have earned their tour memberships at the National Qualifying Schools. These sessions answer many of the questions of a tour rookie.

> **HINT:** Make being a part of the gallery at a PGA Tour event easier with savings on the price of daily or weekly tickets to select PGA, Champions, or Nationwide Tour events. Periodically the Tour partners with other organizations to offer tickets at special prices. One source to check for great discounts is the American Automobile Association (AAA).

Insider Tips for Surviving Tournament Week

1. Remember that you are there to play golf. Participate in the events of sponsors as needed, but do not be distracted by planned social outings or entertainment.

2. Take advantage of the food service offered in the player's lounge. It is good quality, convenient and free.

3. Check the events scheduled for the golf course and plan your practice rounds accordingly. It does you no good to plan to play the course on Tuesday afternoon, if that is when the sponsor has scheduled a shoot-out as an event of the tournament.

4. If you cannot play a course in advance, at least walk the course so that you have seen and studied the holes.

5. Do your laundry regularly. You do not want to be stuck in the hotel laundry room or trying to get your slacks from the local dry cleaner on an afternoon you need to spend on the practice range.

6.   If you are not provided a courtesy car and there is a hotel on property at the golf course, consider staying there. While the daily room rate may be higher than other hotels, if it prevents you from needing a rental car, it may be a cost saver. It will definitely be a time saver.

7.   The equipment trailers at a tournament leave the event the day before the first round. (They need the extra time to drive to the next tournament location.) If you need club repair or club adjustments, get it done early in the week.

8.   Make sure you and your caddie agree on his fee, before you begin to play. The caddie may expect extra pay for the ProAm or he may consider that he or she has been hired to assist in all the events of the week. More on the player-caddie relationship, including rates of pay, is in the next section.

9.   Be prepared to tip the locker room attendant at the end of the tournament. The PGA Tour requires you tip $50 minimum.

10.   If you will be arriving late in the week for the tournament, be sure your equipment representative knows. He can leave a courtesy supply of golf balls for you, even if he has left the tournament before you arrive.

4. Other Opportunities

There is no substitute for tournament competition. Until you make your way onto one of the major golf tours – you must play somewhere. You must play often, and you must test your skills against those of other good players.

In this chapter you will learn about the many opportunities for you to play professional golf outside of the major tours, including developmental tours (also known as mini tours) and international tours. You will also find good advice on part-time professional golf and related golf careers. Both prize money and membership fees vary from year to year for most tours. Contact each tour directly for the most current information.

4.1 The Developmental or Mini Tours

The need to develop a player's game and his or her ability to play tournament golf gave birth to the mini tours or the developmental tours.

4.1.1 The NGA Hooters Tour

The well-known NGA (National Golf Association) Hooter's Tour runs professional 72 hole events (four 18 hole rounds) by the same format as the PGA and Nationwide Tours. They define their tour as a developmental tour because they provide tournament week activities, a diversity of courses and PGA and USGA certified officials, in a similar format to the PGA and Nationwide Tours. Their goal is to provide a place for players to develop into tomorrow's winners on the PGA and Nationwide Tours.

Tournament purses range between $105,000 and $120,000, with each tournament winner taking home approximately $20,000 - $22,000 (payout to 60 and ties). Currently, the leading money winner on the NGA Tour has earned over $750,000 in less than four years of competitive play.

The NGA conducts Ranking Schools for the NGA Hooters Tour. On this tour if you sign up for the Ranking School, you automatically become a member of the NGA Tour. Based on your performance in the

Ranking School, you receive a ranking number. This number determines when during the year you will become eligible to play with exempt status. Past champions from the last two years and Top 100 from the previous year's Money list are exempt from attending the Ranking School.

In order to participate in a Hooters NGA Ranking School, a player must:

- Pay the $2,000 membership fee

- Complete an application form, available through the tour or downloadable from their website at **www.ngahooterstour.com/ application.html**

Entry into Tournaments

The entry fee into each tournament is approximately $650 per tournament. Players should plan for about $400 each week in travel expenses as well. It is not necessary to attend the Hooter's Tour Ranking School in order to play this tour. You may Monday Qualify for tournaments. Winning a tournament for which you have Monday Qualified automatically makes you eligible for all other tour events for the remainder of the season. A Top 20 finish will make you eligible for the tournament the following week. Any qualifier accumulating a minimum of $4,000 in earnings receives tour membership.

To learn more, contact the tour or visit their website.

NGA Hooters Tour
1211 Highway 17 North
North Myrtle Beach, South Carolina 29582
Phone: 800-992-8748
www.ngahooterstour.com

4.1.2 The Tight Lies Tour

One excellent place to play professional golf is on the Tight Lies Tour. Based in Carrolton, Texas, this tour plays tournaments in Texas, Mississippi, and Louisiana, and occasionally other southern or western venues. Their playing season runs April through October with approximately 20 tournaments. Events are primarily four-round tournaments with a cut after 36 holes. They are open to members first, with non-members included on a space-available basis.

Tight Lies events offer no purses below $102,000, with first place paying $20,000 and last paid place averaging about $750.

There is no Qualifying School to gain membership on the Tight Lies Tour. To many players this is a giant "plus". It spares them the fees of the school and it keeps one week of play from determining a player's playing status for an entire golf season.

Requirements for Membership

- Be 18 years of age or older

- Amateurs must have a demonstrated handicap of five or less

- Submit a membership application by the deadline, including a signed Player Agreement and Media Form

- Pay membership fee of approximately $1200 annually for new members or $900 for members returning from the previous year

- Be of good moral character

Tournament participants play in ProAms at most tournaments and may participate in other sponsor events. The Tight Lies Tour considers that it is a very important part of player development for them to learn to interact with sponsors and gain self-assurance in responding to the press – particularly at the end of a rough day!

The Tight Lies Tour sees many young players and a few seasoned golfers. Some tour members are former students who played on college golf teams while others turned pro after high school. This tour even offers a special membership plan that fits into most college summer breaks, for players who are still enrolled in college and wish to play as amateurs during the summer schedule.

Because this is a mini tour, do not think that the competition is second-rate. This tour has been an entry point to the PGA or Champions Tours for many players, including Harrison Frazar, Kelly Grunewald,

Cameron Beckman, Hunter Haas, Brian Wilson, J.L. Lewis, Tim Herron, Jesse Patino, and Steve Veriato. More than 50 Tight Lies members have earned privileges on the Nationwide Tour.

This tour takes pride in preparing players for the PGA and Nationwide Tours. Since all of the events are open to women, it could prepare players for the LPGA and the Futures Tour, but long hitting female players must bring their top game. While the Tight Lies Tour is one of the few men's tours to permit women players, during tournaments, women must play from the same tee boxes as the men play.

> HINT: A bonus for players on the Tight Lies Tour is the Tight Lies
>   Repair Trailer sponsored by Adams Golf. Manned by a
>   PGA Tour veteran who offers club repair, club adjustment,
>   great stories, and sage advice on clubs, players benefit
>   significantly from his onsite service and expertise.

Tight Lies Tour
Post Office Box 112596
Carrollton, Texas 75011-2596
Phone: 972-323-6068
Email: gary@texassportsgroup.com
www.tightliestour.net

4.1.3 Moonlight Golf Tour

An extremely flexible tour for playing professional golf is the Moonlight Tour based in central Florida. This tour program is multi-stage and includes the: Moonlight Tour, NEXT Tour, and Liberty Tour.

The Moonlight Tour offers players digital imagery of their swings for self and peer evaluation, low cost tournament fees and annual membership fees, and 275 days of tournament play each year.

These tournaments are easy to enter, costing only between approximately $60 to $80 for each Moonlight event, and only $100 for annual membership fees. They are an affordable way to keep playing competitive golf, and players who finish in the top 25% on the Moonlight Tour are eligible to play in NEXT tournaments where the prize money is greater. The Moonlight Tour is open to women and amateurs, and has a division for senior players.

As the name implies, the professional or amateur who is "moonlighting" in another job while he or she develops competitive golf skills is often the competitor on the Moonlight Tour. The Tour is committed to keeping entry fees as low-priced as possible and offering opportunities for developing golfers.

Frank McGee, President of the Moonlight Tour reminds players,

"The reward of great golf is great golf itself and those who come to understand this realize that the climb is the excitement."

To learn more contact the tour or visit their website.

Moonlight Golf Association, Inc.
No Exemptions Tour, Inc. (NEXT)
P.O. Box 4232
Seminole, Florida 33775
Phone: 727-393-8531
www.moonlightgolf.com

4.1.4 Additional Developmental or Mini Tours

The following is a partial list of some other strong mini or developmental tours. To learn more about any of these tours contact them or visit their website.

The Allstar Golf Tour (AGT)

Based in Florida, the Allstar Golf Tour offers professionals an opportunity during the winter months of December through February to stay, practice, and compete all in one city. All events are played in the Greater Jacksonville area. The Tour offers a package of unlimited practice during the season, plus many options for living accommodations, and discounts on entry fees.

Allstar Golf Tour
3804 Olympic Lane
Jacksonville, Florida 32223
Phone: (toll free) 877-896-0101
Phone: 904-260-9046
www.allstargolf.cc

Atlantic Coast Golf Tour

Formerly known as the Triangle Golf Tour, this Tour is a proving ground for aspiring PGA and Champions Tour Professionals, including 2002 Q School graduate, Carl Petterson (who placed 2nd in the 2003 Buick Invitational) and Champions Tour veterans, Walter Hall and Terry Mauney.

The Atlantic Coast Golf Tour plays approximately twenty 54-hole events in North Carolina, South Carolina, and Virginia each playing season and offers a special division for professional players ages 40 and older.

> Atlantic Coast Golf Tour
> Post Office Box 2290
> Burlington, North Carolina 27216-2290
> Fax: 919-620-6810
> Email: info@AtlanticCoastGolfTour.com
> **www.atlanticcoastgolftour.com**

Cascade Golf Tour

Each season the Cascade Tour plays approximately 15 events in the Pacific Northwest.

> Cascade Golf Tour
> 418 Frederick St. S.E.
> Olympia, Washington 98501
> Phone: 360-786-8486
> Email: oneill@cascadegolftour.com
> **www.cascadegolftour.com**

The DP Tour (Developing Professionals)

This tour plays events in Georgia, Alabama, Tennessee, and South Carolina. Fully exempt members of the PGA or Nationwide Tours are not eligible to play in DP events.

> The DP Tour
> 7005 Longleaf Creek Drive
> Pensacola, Florida 32526
> Phone: 888-422-4734 or 850-944-8944

Email: slocumk@bellsouth.net
www.dptour.com

The Golden Bear Tour

Founded by Jack Nicklaus, The Golden Bear Tour is a south Florida mini tour on which top players can earn serious prize money. In the 2002 season this tour's leading money winner won over $120,000 in prize money, while 20 other top Golden Bear players won between $30,000 and $100,000 from their efforts.

Before you decide that this is the tour for you, consider that the individual membership fee is over $17,000 annually and only those players finishing roughly in the top 50 will break even on their investment. On the other hand, because all events are played within a one-hour drive of West Palm Beach, Florida, if you can reside in the area during the four and a half month playing season, you will have very limited tournament travel expenses. Members of the Golden Bear Tour can play in approximately 14 events and in each one have a shot at the $25,000+ first place prize money.

Golden Bear Tour
11770 U.S. Highway One, #100
North Palm Beach, Florida 33408
Phone: 561-626-5999
www.goldenbeartour.com

Golden State Tour

Golden State Tour is the United States' largest and oldest mini tour. Events are open to professionals, amateurs, and seniors. Steve Pate, Kirk Triplett, and Duffy Waldorf are among this California tour's many graduates to the PGA and Nationwide Tours.

Golden State Golf Tour Inc.
P.O. Box 710
Pauma Valley, California 92061-0710
Phone: 760-742-1461
Fax: 760-742-1915
Email: gstour@gstour.com
www.gstour.com

Integrity Golf Tour

The IGT plays competitive tournament golf throughout the southwestern and central United States. Their events are open to anyone with a handicap of 26 or lower. Fees vary from approximately $50 to $500 per event.

Integrity Golf Tour
www.integritygolftour.com

Contact information by region:

New Mexico and Southern California
Phone: 480-699-8792
Email: igtofphoenix@aol.com

Southern Nevada and Central California
Phone: 702-269-7520
Email: donl@lvcm.com

Northern Nevada and Northern California
Phone: 702-346-5680 or 702-346-5094

Arkansas, Oklahoma, Texas, and Louisiana
Phone: 405-329-2572 or 800 627-5544
Email: phil@hmtins.com

Colorado
Phone: 970-963-6369
Email: Cunninghamgolf@hotmail.com

Utah
Phone: 435-652-8565
Email: IGT_1@msn.com

Illinois and Wisconsin
Phone: 847-691-2059
Email: igt_n_illinois@yahoo.com

Mid Florida Golf Tour, Inc.

This tour offers guaranteed first place prize money of $1,000 in all events with 25 players or more. As a special opportunity for Junior and Amateur players, one-day events can be entered for as little as $75, offering an excellent chance for players to retain their amateur status while competing with pros. An official handicap of 8 or lower is required of all competitors. The Mid Florida Golf Tour features events for men, ladies, and seniors, plus amateur-only tournaments.

Mid Florida Golf Tour, Inc.
PO Box 61313
Palm Bay, Florida 32906
Phone: 321-953-2247
Fax: 775-458-1961
Email: golftour@aol.com
www.midfloridagolftour.com

National Competitive Golf Tour

National Competitive Golf Tour events are played in three divisions to guarantee payout and ensure fairness for players at all levels. Most events include:

- **A Net Division** – Players compete using their official handicaps.

- **A Gross Division** – Players compete straight up; no handicaps are used and every player in the field is competing against the best players in the event.

- **A Pro Only Division** – Competition is straight up from the championship (or Tour) tees. Club professionals and touring pros take advantage of head to head competition with guaranteed purses.

National Competitive Golf Tour
www.ncgtour.com

National Competitive Golf Tour
Eastland Professional Suites
1404 Eastland Dr.
Bloomington, Illinois 61701
Phone: 309-452-0217
Fax: 309-888-2793
Email: Mike@ncgtour.com

Florida
National Competitive Golf Tour
6679 Meandering Way
Bradenton, Florida 34202
Phone: 877-766-4626
Fax: 877-844-4653
Email: Tim@ncgtour.com

Louisiana
National Competitive Golf Tour
2205 Landau Lane
Bossier City, Louisiana 71111
Phone: 318-424-4868
Fax: 318-675-0202
Email: Terry@ncgtour.com

Pepsi Tour

The Pepsi Tour plays events in California, Arizona, and Nevada. In 2001, the tour hosted over 100 events and paid over $1 million dollars in total prize money. Some events include Senior and Ladies divisions.

Pepsi Tour
All Golfers Tour Association
14272 Wicks Blvd.
San Leandro, California 94577
Phone: 800-614-Golf
Fax: 510-352-6658
Email: pepsitour@earthlink.net
www.pepsitour.com

4.2 Playing International Tours

One option for golfers who have not quite found their place on the US golf tours is to play a professional tour in another country – referred to in the American golf world as the international tours. International tours have extremely talented players but sometimes the overall competition is not as tough as in the US.

Playing on a tour in another country gives you the opportunity to earn money while playing professional golf. You can improve your game with tournament competition and experience world travel and new cultures. If you play well, your game may find a permanent home on a foreign tour or you may discover that you are ready to face the challenge of the US Tours.

> **EXAMPLE:** US PGA Tour player, Corey Pavin began his career path in professional golf by playing on international tours. Included in his international tournament wins are the German Open, the Tokai Classic in Japan, the Asian Masters, the South Africa PGA Championship, and the New Zealand Open. Pavin returned to play the US PGA Tour, where he has won 14 PGA Tour events along with having won the US Open, and played on the Ryder Cup and President's Cup teams.

4.2.1 World Golf Championships

The World Golf Championships are events of the International Federation of PGA Tours. The Federation, founded in 1996, has two main objectives:

- To organize world championship competitions for leading players

- To maintain the official standard for determining worldwide ranking of players

The Federation brings golf's international best together to play. It lets players compare themselves with other players globally, and it raises the standard for competition on all its member tours (see the next section for information about member tours).

Held at varying outstanding courses around the world, roughly one half of the World Golf Championship events are in the United States. They include:

- Accenture Match Play Championship

- NEC Invitational

- American Express Championship

- The EMC World Cup

For more information about the World Golf Championships visit their website at **www.worldgolfchampionships.com**.

4.2.2 International Tours

Around the world there are six tours organized collectively as the International Federation of PGA Tours. These tours represent the top competition in worldwide golf. The US PGA Tour, along with the European Tour, Asian PGA Tour, Japan Golf Tour, Southern Africa PGA Tour, and the PGA Tour of Australasia are the governing bodies of the International Federation of PGA Tours. The Canadian Tour currently holds associate membership in the Federation.

Players who finish first, second, or third on the European, Australasian and Japanese Tours are exempt from the first two stages of qualifiers at the US PGA Tour Q School. Players who finish fourth, fifth or sixth are exempt from only the first stage of qualifying in Q School. Under consideration for the future is giving exemption into the second stage of the US PGA Tour Q School to leading players from the Canadian, Asian, and South Africa Tours. These options for exemptions are another benefit of playing one of the international tours.

Like the US PGA Tour, each of the Federation members runs their own competitive season of events and qualifying schools. For information on membership requirements, tournament schedules, and other important facts, contact each tour of the Federation directly. Mail, fax, or email is recommended. On the golf course, the game of golf is a universal language, but if you contact some of the international offices by phone, you may not find anyone who speaks English.

European Tour

The European Tour is comprised of three tours: the European Tour, SR. European Tour, and the Challenge Tour.

> European Tour
> Wentworth Club, Wentworth Drive
> Virginia Water, Surrey
> GU25 4LX
> England
> Phone: +44 (0) 1344 840400
> Fax: +44 (0) 1344 840500
> **www.europeantour.com**

For women seeking to play internationally there is the Evian Ladies European Tour (LET), a tour that is rapidly growing in both fan-popularity and in player talent.

> Ladies European Tour
> The Tytherington Club
> The Old Hall
> Macclesfield, Cheshire
> SK10 2LQ
> England
> Phone: +44 (0)1625 611444
> Fax: +44 (0)1625 610406
> Email: mail@ladieseuropeantour.com
> **www.ladieseuropeantour.com**

Asian PGA Tour

The Asian PGA Tour is also called the Davidoff Tour for their corporate sponsor, Davidoff Café.

> Asian PGA Tour
> APAG Berhad
> 415/416 Block A, Kelana Business Center
> 97, Jalan SS 7/2 Kelana Jaya
> Selangor, Malaysia
> **www.asianpga.com**

Japan Golf Tour

Japan offers the Japan LPGA Tour and a well-established Senior professional golf tour in addition to its regular tour. (The Japan Golf Tour website is in Japanese, but sections are available in English.)

> Japan Golf Tour
> 1-3-5 Akasaka, Minato ku
> Tokyo, Japan P.C. 107-0052
> **www.jgto.org**

Southern Africa PGA Tour

The Southern Africa PGA Tour has a well-established Senior professional golf tour and a women's tour, in addition to their regular tours.

> Southern Africa PGA Tour
> P.O. Box 1532
> Somerset West, 7129
> Republic of South Africa
> Phone: +27 21 850 6500
> Fax: +27 21 852 8271
> Email: media@sunshinetour.com
> **www.sunshinetour.com**

> Women's Professional Golf Association of South Africa
> P.O. Box 72275
> Parkview, 2122
> Republic of South Africa
> Fax: (Lesley) +27 11 646-5715
> Email: lesleyc@worldonline.co.za
> **www.wpga.co.za**

PGA Tour of Australasia

> PGA Tour of Australasia
> Suite 302, 77 Berry Street
> North Sydney 2060
> NSW, Australia
> **www.pgatour.com.au**

Australian Ladies Professional Golf Association
PO Box 447
Mudgeeraba QLD 4213
Phone: +61 (0) 755 929 343
Fax: +61 (0) 755 929 344
Email: info@alpgtour.com
www.alpgatour.com

Another Helpful Resource

For information about golf in the United Kingdom, contact:

PGA (of the United Kingdom)

Professional Golfers Association (of the United Kingdom)
Centenary House
The Belfry
Sutton Coldfield, West Midlands
B76 9PT
Phone: +44 01675 470333
Fax: +44 01675 477888
www.pga.org.uk

4.2.3 The Canadian Tour

The Canadian Tour is an international tour option geographically well situated for most US players. In fact, it plays so close to home that some events are held in South Carolina, Texas, Arizona, and Florida.

Playing this tour has made a great career beginning for many professional golfers, preparing them for bigger tours with larger prize money. Many players play both the Canadian Tour and the Nationwide Tour during the same season or play the Canadian Tour for a few seasons, and then move on to play the Nationwide or the PGA Tour. Each year roughly ten Canadian Tour veterans gain membership on the PGA or Nationwide Tour at the Qualifying Schools for those tours.

Marty Henwood, Communications Director for the Tour, offers rookie players this advice:

"When you are ready to move from amateur status to professional, pick a tour that will ready you with week-in, week-out experiences, where you can spend a season or two and then be prepared to move on to the PGA, Nationwide, or European Tour."

Over 200 professional golfers are members of the Canadian Tour; slightly less than half of them are Canadian. This produces tournament fields that are an international mix of aspiring players and professional golf veterans.

Here is a partial list of US PGA Tour golfers who played the Canadian Tour: Stuart Appleby, Notah Begay III, Robert Damron, Chris DiMarco, Dan Halldorson, Tim Herron, Steve Stricker, Kirk Triplett, Mike Weir and Richard Zokol.

In 2002, the Canadian Tour played a total of 19 tournaments in four countries, including four events played in the US. Under a long-term contract, The Golf Channel broadcasts at least six Canadian Tour events. Thanks in part to committed corporate sponsors including Telus and MTS, prize money on the Canadian Tour reached almost $3 million Canadian dollars in their most recent playing season.

Tournament weeks include one ProAm, and social and recreational activities planned for the players at each tournament venue. Players are paid for their ProAm participation.

USGA rules govern Canadian Tour events whether played in the US or in Canada. Most of the Tour's tournament formats are four 18-hole rounds with a cut after 36 holes to the low scoring 60 players and ties. All players making the cut in the tournament receive a prize check, with the last tournament position paid receiving (in Canadian dollars) approximately $150 to $300, and the winner receiving approximately $22,000 to $30,000. Prize money varies because of the size of each tournament purse and the number of players who make the cut.

Monday Qualifying is a way into Canadian Tour events or you may attempt to gain tour membership at one of the three annual Qualifying Schools for the tour. At least one of the Qualifying Schools is held in the United States.

Q-School fees are approximately $1,970 (or $1,250 US dollars) plus an additional $470 (or $300 US dollars) membership fee for the players who qualify at the school. Entry fees to individual Canadian Tournaments are approximately $212 ($135 US dollars) per event.

During each season, player standings are ranked on the McDonald's Order of Merit, which is the official money list of the tour. Over thirty players will have season winnings of $20,000 or more, with the top money winners (typically two or three players) winning more than $70,000 in prize money.

Like their US counterparts, the Canadian Tour and the Canadian Professional Golf Association (CPGA) are separate organizations. The Canadian Tour is the membership of touring professional players, while the CPGA governs Canadian golf club professionals.

To learn more about Monday Qualifying, the Canadian Tour Q School, or specific information on their requirements for membership, contact the Canadian Tour.

Canadian Tour
212 King Street West, Suite 203
Toronto, Ontario M5H 1K5
Canada
Phone: 416-204-1564
Fax: 416-204-1368

To follow the players, schedules, and stats of the Canadian Tour, visit the website at **www.cantour.com**.

Other informative websites for Canadian golf include:

Canadian Golf
www.cangolf.com

Canadian Professional Golfers Association
www.cpga.com

Interesting Note About Canadian Golf

Canadian Mike Weir, winner of the 2003 Masters, the 2003 Bob Hope Chrysler Classic, the 2003 Nissan Open, the 2001 Tour Championship, the World Golf American Express Championship and two-time winner of the Air Canada Championship, is one of the PGA Tour 's few left-handed players.

With Mike Weir, Phil Mickelson, and the Champion's Tour's Bob Charles as exceptions, most professional golf lefties play right-handed. Except in Canada.

Canada has many more left-handed golfers, both professional and amateur, than does the US.

Why? The reason is hockey. Children in Canada who learn to play hockey (which most do) learn to use their hockey sticks as adeptly when swinging to their left as to their right. If they later take up golf, they may choose to be right-handed players or they may be so comfortable with swinging from the left that it carries over to their golf game.

4.3 Amateur Golf

If you plan to play professionally and you are not ready to try the tours and mini tours, then you must play competitive amateur golf. If you are a young player, playing amateur golf permits you to maintain your eligibility for college scholarships, and allows you and your game time to mature. Until you are 100% ready to compete as a pro, remain an amateur. Outside of the PGA or LPGA Tours, amateur golf offers some of the toughest competition, and an excellent place to sharpen your skills at tournament play.

Amateur golf is the heart and soul of the game of golf. It is also the US Amateur, the US Ladies Amateur, the US Senior Amateur, the prestigious British Amateur, the Walker Cup, and a host of events all offering tough playing fields of highly skilled competitive golfers.

The rules for maintaining amateur status are very specific and include more than just the issue of playing golf for money. Playing for prizes, endorsing a product (even if you are not paid to make the endorsement) or receiving payment to teach golf, are all actions that can cost a player his or her amateur status. To further complicate matters, the guidelines for amateur status by the USGA are different from the NCAA guidelines for player eligibility. If you are an amateur player and you are hoping to receive a college golf scholarship, then you must meet the guidelines of both the USGA and the NCAA.

> **HINT:** NCAA rules do not prohibit you from talking to a sports agent, however you can jeopardize your college eligibility and your amateur status if you agree to agent representation – even if it is only a verbal agreement and it does not go into effect until you have completed high school or college.

Following are web addresses for more information about amateur events. You can find the 10 national amateur championships at the USGA website, along with a link to the current year's Directory of Amateur Tournament Golf.

USGA Championships
www.usga.org/champs

The US Amateur
www.usamateur.org

Royal and Ancient: Amateur Event Entry Forms
www.randa.

The Walker Cup
www.walkercup.org

The Royal Canadian Golf Association (RCGA) is the governing body of Canadian amateur golf. The RCGA conducts the Bell Canadian Open, the AT&T Senior PGA Tour stop, and the Bank of Montreal Canadian Women's Open.

Royal Canadian Golf Association
www.rcga.org

4.4 Part-time Professional Golf

Your image of a professional golfer may be David Duval or Phil Mickelson climbing into a private jet and heading off – with devoted staff around him – for another glamorous golf resort. But, in your pursuit of golfing gold, this lifestyle may not happen quickly for you. It may not happen at all. Still, there are other ways to be a professional golfer.

Success in professional golf remains a mysterious synchronization of your best play at a time you are most physically fit, mentally composed, and sufficiently funded to break into the top levels of the game. In case you are in the majority, and this does not happen for you – you do not have to give up your dream. Re-think what professional golf means.

If you accept prize money (or gifts over a certain value) for your play, then you are a professional golfer. Somewhere between the player in his private jet and the player who never plays for more than a trophy at the club championship, there are successful compromises. Compromise does not have to mean giving in or giving up. Compromise can mean accomplishing your goal while working around the challenges.

Before you throw in your golf towel, consider some options for successful compromise:

- Develop a career as a golf teacher in an area such as Florida or south Texas, where the winter months are the busiest golf season. You will have the chance to work long hours in the tourist season of December through March. About the time your employer is ready to cut-back his teaching staff each spring as business slows, you will be ready to play a mini tour season or try Monday Qualifying for tougher events.

- Reside in an area that offers frequent mini tour events, and then depend on a career other than professional golf for your primary income. Do anything that pays the bills from Monday thru Friday. But play golf for prize money on Saturday and Sunday, and you are a professional golfer.

- Work in a career that offers seasonal employment around the schedule of a tour you wish to play. A construction job in the summer may be just what you need to build your strength, stamina and bank account, before you head south of the equator for the Southern African or Australasian Tours, or even to a Florida winter tour.

- Plan ahead to have a second career. Earn a living, raise a family, build a retirement nest egg, but when you reach 50 years old, take a stab at getting on the Champions Tour.

If you really want to play golf professionally, be receptive to looking at all of your options. Combining two careers is not easy. It may always leave you feeling as if you do not do justice to either one. In addition, the plan that works for you for two, five or ten years of your life may not be one you follow forever.

But do not limit yourself to the idea that professional golf has to be an all or nothing career.

If you can find a way that is comfortable for you to earn a living yet still enjoy the competition, the experience and the prize money of part-time tournament golf, then you are not only a professional golfer, you are a successful professional golfer.

4.5 Related Golf Careers

As you play competitive golf, you may discover that you enjoy other aspects about the game more than the constant travel, unending practice, uncertain payoffs, and nerve wracking competition – that is, being a professional player. Your love of the game, but dislike of the lifestyle could lead you to one of the related careers of the golf industry and a chance to spend your workday at a golf course! Consider some of the related careers and their typical benefits.

HINT: You can find jobs through many of the resources listed in this guide. You may also be able to find some positions posted online. The following websites have information about job openings that you can access for a fee.

USGolfJobs.com
www.usgolfjobs.com

Golfing Careers
www.golfingcareers.com

4.5.1 Golf Pro

Another option for playing golf professionally is to become a golf pro. The PGA of America (remember, it is not part of the PGA Tour) is the organization that trains and prepares most golf pros in the US. Currently there are approximately 17,000 golf facilities and over half of them employ staff trained by the PGA of America.

Section 2.4 discussed the PGA-PGM college degree program of the PGA of America. There are other levels of certification available from the PGA of America. These certifications require a combination of workshops, self-study, testing, and apprenticeships, but do not require you attend college.

The Golf Professional Training Program (GPTP) prepares you for most jobs at a golf course, as well as for teaching golf. The program is tiered so you may choose the number of levels you wish to complete, or complete them all. One of the many benefits of the PGA of America's program is that it will permit you to play as a professional in PGA of America tournaments.

A PGA of America Section represents each geographic region of the country. There are 41 sections in the US and each regularly hosts competitive professional tournaments for their golf professionals and Class A teaching pros. Additionally, in most PGA Tour tournaments, a playing spot goes to the winner of a local PGA of America Sectional tournament. As a PGA of America member, sectional tournaments give you the opportunity to play regular tournament golf for prize money, and to potentially gain a spot in a PGA Tour event.

The website of the PGA of America is detailed and informative. It includes a self-assessment quiz, information on their certificated and degreed programs, requirements, employment opportunities, and program costs. Visit the PGA of America at **www.pga.com**.

4.5.2 Other Golf Careers

Tournaments

Tournament jobs permit you to enjoy firsthand the excitement of professional events, have a close-up look at the players at work, and give you some off-course opportunities to mix and mingle with the players and their families. A tournament job may require a specialized college degree, such as marketing, but you can sometimes work your way into these jobs without a degree or with only some college training.

Start as an outstanding tournament volunteer and make sure that the tournament management staff knows of your interest in a paid position. You may have to work your way up through the ranks of tournament responsibilities, but what a great way to learn all the ins and outs of golf tournaments.

Golf Equipment

Companies that manufacture golf equipment hire employees:

- to design and test clubs and balls

- to sell the product to retailers (including sports equipment stores and pro shops)

- to take care of the equipment needs of tour players who are constantly looking for better products and a playing edge

You can gain skills as a clubmaker by apprenticing with an established club craftsman, through classes for a PGA of America certification or at a private golf school. However, you will almost always need a degree, typically in mechanical engineering or physics, to move into the upper levels of product research and design.

When golf equipment companies hire sales or player relations staffs, they look for individuals with college degrees in sports marketing or business and an in-depth understanding of the game. Sometimes a professional player will spend a few years playing then move into this type of job. With or without a college degree, however, expect to need basic computer skills for tracking inventory and maintaining other records.

Pro Shops

The pro shop at a golf course is a mini-department store devoted to golf. Typically the pro shop sells golf clothing, golf equipment, shoes, gloves, bags, possibly golf books, and sometimes golf décor items like clocks or desk sets. A pro shop may be responsible for club and shoe rentals, club fittings, and booking tee times and lessons.

Managers and staff of the pro shop need backgrounds in retail sales, merchandising, ordering, and inventory, along with thorough knowledge of the game. People hired as managers usually have college or golf school training and may be PGA of America certified, but it is possible to work into these jobs simply by starting as a sales or inventory clerk and working up the ladder.

If you work in a pro shop you usually enjoy discounted rates for playing, practicing, lessons, and for golf merchandise. It is another great way to spend your day at a golf course without your income depending on what you score.

A comprehensive database of golf courses, both US and international destinations, is available at **www.golfcourse.com**. This helpful website includes contact information, course ratings, pro shop offerings and much more.

Golf Course Architecture/Golf Course Design

Designing or constructing golf courses can be fascinating careers. Either career requires hands-on experience in golf, or construction, and usually both. You cannot be a "walk-on" in these fields, but some professional players without construction experience have become successful golf course architects by working in partnership with an experienced golf course construction company.

To find out more about the art and skill of aesthetically fitting four par 3's, four par 5's, and ten par 4's into a piece of land, while complying with all environmental and building permits, keeping workers motivated and owners happy, and staying on a timetable and budget, read about some of golf's most respected designers.

> The American Society of Golf Course Architects
> **www.golfdesign.org**

> VonHagge, Smelek and Baril
> Premiere Global Golf Course Architects
> **www.vonhagge.com**

Golf Course Maintenance

Jobs in golf course maintenance include everything from the person riding the mower to the Golf Course Superintendent. Some of these jobs require only the desire to work hard in the fresh air and sunshine. Others call for certification in areas of turf grass management or certifications in handling of chemicals, and still some require specialized four-year degrees.

You can complete some turf grass courses entirely through a distance education study (online or email studies). The University of Georgia is one school with such a program. Visit the Principles of Turfgrass Management website at **www.gactr.uga.edu/is/turf/index.html**.

The Golf Course Superintendents Association of America (GCSAA) endorses the University of Georgia's ten-month turfgrass management certificate. Visit **www.gcsaa.com** for a comprehensive site with more information on careers in golf course maintenance, including job postings, sample job descriptions, salary information, and even tips for your job interview.

Golf Course Staff

Golf courses are considered part of the hospitality industry. If located at a resort, they may include hotel and convention facilities. They generally have food service, some with high quality dining. Like most businesses, they employ people in administrative and secretarial positions, accounting, human resources, marketing, maintenance, and security.

While none of these jobs puts you on the golf course, they all enable you to work in a golf course environment and stay in touch with the game. Most of the time, they include employee discounts on play, practice, lessons, and merchandise. And, when you knock off work at the end of the day, you could not be in a better spot for hitting a few buckets of balls on the range or perhaps working in 18 holes.

4.5.3 Internships

The USGA Foundation (the philanthropic arm of the USGA) underwrites an excellent internship program. Each year they help make available approximately 100 paid internships. These opportunities, all part of the P.J. Boatwright, Jr. Internship Program, vary in length, assignment and responsibilities. Most are programs designed by state and regional golf associations and include a monthly stipend of about $1,500, plus travel expenses. Requirements include you having specific, serious interest in golf and sometimes, but not always, call for you to be a recent college graduate.

None of these internships focuses on playing golf as a professional. They do not improve or increase playing skills or playing opportunities. They do however, provide the chance to get first-hand experience in other areas of the golf industry, often by working in tournament operations, tournament administration or Junior golf programs.

Different associations design each internship, and each offers a different experience. If you think you may have the right qualifications and are interested in a three, six, or even a 12-month program, you must contact the sponsoring golf association directly.

Visit the USGA's website at **www.usga.org/foundation** to find the complete list of all internships and names of who to contact. Some of the addresses include links to additional information, but most require that you contact the organization's headquarters. Telephone first to request the full description of any internship in which you are particularly interested, then include a cover letter and résumé with your application.

You will also find the other employment postings of the USGA, as well as information on the Foundation's Fellowship program for individuals interested in a professional position and growth experience in administration of not-for-profit golf organization.

5. Your Team

As a professional golfer, you are self-employed. You work for yourself. You do not work for the PGA Tour or any other professional tour to which you belong. The product you sell is your own accomplished golfing skills. Ironically, you are the boss, the product, and your own advertisement.

However, you don't do it alone. To become a successful professional golfer you need the support of other people. In this chapter you will learn more about some people who can help you achieve your goals.

5.1 Agents

5.1.1 Getting An Agent

Rookies in professional sports often ask, "How do I find an agent?" The answer is, you don't. Agents have a way of finding you. Professional sports agents keep tabs on players with promising careers. They will recognize when your career becomes marketable and ready for an agent probably before you will.

Knowing that an agent will find you when the time is right, however, does not completely leave you without a role in the process. If you are a superstar at your local club, but never compete against professional players, such as those on the Nationwide Tour, Canadian Tour, Tight Lies Tour, Hooters Tour, or other strong mini tour, then agents will not know about your game.

Do not expect an agent to find you on the back nine of your hometown golf course. You have to be playing in tournaments against players of established skill for an agent to take interest in your career. Golf is never just about your great game; you are always measured against the rest of the playing field.

When your career is right for an agent, the agent will probably make contact with you at a tournament or tour event, perhaps through casual conversations while you are on the practice tee. He or she will try to arrange a time to meet privately with you, typically over lunch or dinner. Expect this meeting to include a pitch for potential services to you. The agent may bring you a written proposal showing earnings projections he believes he can generate for you from off-course sources (any source other than tournament winnings). Be prepared for him to have a written contract in hand.

Do not sign this contract. If your career has reached the point that one agent is interested in you, others will be as well. Step back, rent a video of *Jerry McGuire* and listen to Tom Cruise and Cuba Gooding Jr. shout, "Show me the money!" Then go comparison shop for an agent and a contract before you make your decision.

5.1.2 Who's Who in the Agent Business

Look for an individual or a company that has a reputation of success with representing other players. Consider how long an agent has been in the business and who he already represents. Ask around. Lastly, it is very important to find an agent who shows up regularly at tour events, so seek out a familiar face.

International Management Group (IMG)

Any discussion of sports agents in professional golf typically begins with the International Management Group (IMG). This Cleveland, Ohio based sports marketing agency is the largest and probably the most powerful sports marketing and management company in the world. Their areas of expertise include athlete representation, event management, television production and programming, golf course design and management, marketing and licensing, sports academies, arts, and entertainment.

Founded by business expert Mark McCormack, IMG began their management of clients with Arnold Palmer and a handshake deal. Present or past golf stars they represent include Tiger Woods, David Duval, Mark O'Meara, Colin Montgomerie, Annika Sorenstam, and hundreds of other professional athletes and well-known personalities.

IMG
1360 East 9th Street, Suite 100
Cleveland, Ohio 44114
Phone: 216-522-1200

Some of the other prominent sports management companies, and those on their present or past client lists, include:

Cross Consulting

325 Sharon Park Drive M114
Menlo Park, California 94025
Phone: 559-440-4594
Partial client list: Al Geiberger, Scott McCarron, Dave Stockton

Gaylord Sports Management

14646 N. Kierland Boulevard, Suite 230
Scottsdale, Arizona 85254
Phone: 480-483-9500
Partial client list: Phil Mickelson, Mark Calcavecchia, David Gossett
www.gaylordsports.com

Hambric Sports Management

2515 McKinney Avenue #940
Dallas, Texas 75201
Phone: 214-720-7179
Partial client list: Steve Flesch, Bob Tway, and Brian Claar

Links Management Group

5068 W. Plano Parkway Suite 3000
Plano, Texas 75093
Phone: 972-381-4227
Partial client list: Kenny Perry, Loren Roberts, Trevor Dodds

Octagon

7100 Forest Avenue Suite 201
Richmond, Virginia 23226
Phone: 804-285-4200
Partial client list: Allen Doyle, Justin Leonard, Davis Love, III
www.octagon.com

SFX Sports Group

5335 Wisconsin Avenue NW #850
Washington, DC 20015
Phone: 202-237-0120
Partial client list: Ted Tryba, Scott Verplank, and John Daly
http://sfx.com/publish_static.asp?page=AboutSFXsportsGroup

The agencies listed above have many clients they represent. Another option is to be an agent's only client. Numerous players, especially those with established careers, choose to incorporate their own management company and hire their own promotional staff. Some players have also had success by having a friend or family member who is appropriately skilled in marketing or law act as their agent.

Weigh your options. A large firm generally has established industry contacts, financial depth, and specialists in different aspects of the business. A small company often has lower overhead to support and an opportunity to be very focused on your needs. No two player-agent agreements are the same simply because the needs and careers of every player are different.

5.1.3 Agent Agreements

Some professional golfers have only limited relationships with their agents. In other cases, an agent may be involved in many details of the player's life. Still other players go through their entire careers without having agent representation. As a professional golfer you must consider, if you want an agent, who you will select, and what percentage of your earnings you are willing to relinquish.

Agent commissions range from 10% to 25% of your gross earnings. They occasionally are based on all of your earnings, including your tournament winnings, but this type of agreement is less popular. In recent years, tournament purses have become too large to make it logical for a player to give his agent such a high percentage of his income. Especially when today's professional golfer is likely to have other people, like his coach and his caddie, to whom he is regularly writing hefty checks. Most often, commissionable earnings will include only those earnings from deals initiated by your agent.

An agent should always increase, never decrease, the amount of money you put in your pocket. In a properly structured player-agent agreement, both sides win. But there are variables that will affect this, including how well you continue to play, if you maintain a positive public image, and in the long run, the overall economic climate.

No agent can market you well if your game has gone south, your behavior is so unacceptable a sponsor will not touch you, or the economy is in recession.

Any agreement you sign with an agent is a legally binding contract written by the agent's attorneys to protect the agent. Bad arrangements can be easy to get into and complex and costly to end. In addition, if you have amateur status that you are seeking to protect – perhaps an NCAA golf scholarship on the line – you could blow it all with your signature on the wrong document. Understand what you are signing.

> **HINT:** Advice from other professional golfers and your golf coach can be very helpful, but consider consulting an attorney who specializes in sports contracts before you sign a deal.

Athlete's Guide to Agents by Robert H. Ruxin and Gary Uberstine is a helpful reference with more information on agent agreements.

5.1.4 What Your Agent Will Do for You

The primary role of your agent is to maximize your off-course income through endorsements and appearance fees. Some agents also serve as business managers. They assume responsibility for screening and handling any business tasks that take your time and focus away from play, practice, rest, and relaxation with your family.

If you choose agent representation, one of the first things your agent will do is seek a "niche" for your particular type of image. Some players, like Greg Norman or Ben Crenshaw, may not be at the top of current leader boards, yet they generate huge market recognition from their names alone. Other players, like Vijay Singh, Scott Hoch, or Tom Kite are most marketable for their current or past playing records.

Still others seem to incorporate talent, personality, and appearance into one marketable package. The enduring popularity of Nancy Lopez and Arnold Palmer, neither of whom has won a tournament in years, are excellent examples of this type of persona.

With an angle on your marketable image, your agent will next begin seeking marketing alliances for you within the golf industry. He will approach companies that produce golf equipment, golf apparel, shoes, shafts, and headwear through phone inquires, written proposals, and sales calls. If you have selected an agent who already has strong contacts with these industries, then you are a step ahead.

After a prospective company's representative reviews your bio and meets with your agent, he may want to meet you and perhaps plan a dinner or a round of golf for you and his company executives. Be positive and pleasant with the client. Stay out of the details of negotiating, particularly in front of the potential sponsor. Let your agent do what you hired him or her to do.

As recognition of your name increases, so will your agent's options for finding you additional income sources. Non-golf corporate contracts, like Raymond Floyd's television commercials for Advil or the various players who appear in print advertisements for Rolex, are examples of this type of representation. There may also be opportunities for you to play in overseas tournaments, make personal appearances, or collaborate on books and videotapes.

Another excellent source of off course income is from corporate outings. These are one or two-day events that will require you to give a group lesson, perform a golfing exhibition, or perhaps play a round of golf with the attendees, giving them helpful tips on their game. Your agent may help promote you for corporate outings through a brochure about you that he or his agency has developed. In addition to marketing you and finalizing your outing contract, he may participate in coordinating the overall events of the outing and your itinerary.

Your one-day payment for such appearances can be from $5,000 to $25,000, with the potential to go as high as the $100,000 per day payments some top players earn.

5.2 Sponsors and Clients

Sponsors can be an important part of your team. Some individuals or companies are willing to invest $50,000 to $100,000 or more to cover expenses in a promising golfer's career. Clients are companies that hire you for corporate golf events (see the paragraph above).

As explained in the previous section, an agent can be instrumental in getting you both corporate sponsorships and clients. However, you may decide you do not want agent representation or that you prefer to represent yourself. While this will take time away from your play and practice, there are ways you can increase your own media visibility and your income producing opportunities.

5.2.1 How to Prepare a Résumé

Start by developing a professional résumé (see the sample on the next page). Include your most notable playing experience first and any wins or top finishes you have had in tournaments. List professional, amateur, and collegiate golf events. If you have given golf instruction or taken college courses in marketing or public speaking, be sure to include that, along with copies of any media coverage you may have received.

You may even want to seek quotes about your play from respected sources such as another professional player, sports writer, or golf instructor. These quotes can be included in the résumé you create, perhaps serving as the headlines for your bio sheet.

You can have this résumé or personal profile prepared professionally by an independent publicist or a résumé service. You may have the skills to prepare this yourself. You or a knowledgeable friend can lay-out much of what you need on a home computer and a good copy service or office support business can help you create the finished product. One advantage of preparing your résumé yourself is that you have all the master files and can easily and economically update it as your playing successes expand.

Whether your résumé is one page and a photograph or is a multi-page color file, just make sure that it is neat, well written, thoroughly spell-checked, and reproduced clearly on a high quality paper.

 Above all else, make sure it is accurate. Promote yourself well, but do not stretch the truth. The more well known you become in the future, the more public scrutiny there will be of your past.

5.2.2 Contacting Potential Sponsors and Clients

Once your résumé is complete, use it in the same way an agent would.

To reach clients, mail copies along with a personalized letter to any companies or groups that you think might be interested in a private golf outing or event. Be sure you spell out just what you have in mind to offer them and the fees you expect. If you need to rent space at a golf course to provide the instruction, research cost and availability so that the fees you charge cover your expenses. If the event requires you to travel, make sure both you and your client agree on who is paying your travel costs.

When you send letters seeking sponsorship money, specify how much you need and define your playing goals and objectives. If you are willing to repay a sponsor's investment based on future wins, make that clear too.

The following page features a sample Résumé for a player in the early stages of his or her career.

Mail or deliver your information to any business where you or your family and friends have contacts, and do not forget that the Chamber of Commerce (**www.chamberofcommerce.com**) and even the Yellow Pages can help you identify possible clients.

When you send your information to people you do not know personally, phone ahead and ask the name of the employee to whom you should address your letter. Typically you will be looking for someone in marketing, corporate events, or human resources. Do not overlook professional organizations and clubs as clients for golf events. Just start small. It takes a good bit of work and preparation to sell, organize, and execute your own golf outings and you will learn with each experience.

Sample Resume for Player in Early Stages of Career

Joe Bunkers

Professional Golfer

"Joe Bunkers, possibly the most talented young player
we've seen take on the course at Oakmont "
says Bob Smith, sportswriter for the
Pittsburgh Times, August 11, 2001

Playing Highlights

2003   (T5) Nationwide Tour South Texas Classic

Played in the US OPEN

2002 (T4) Tight Lies Tour Official Money List

Made the cut in four Nationwide Tour events

Monday Qualified for Nationwide Tour seven of eleven tries

2001 Winner, US Public Links Championship

Second Team All-American

All SEC Team, three years

1999 Winner of the Tennessee State Amateur

(T2) Memphis City Classic

Winner Franklin, TN., Junior Golf Classic (3 times)

Additional Facts

Associate Degree in Communications Technology,

University of Tennessee, 2000

Assistant Instructor in NIKE Junior Golf Clinics, 1996-1998

Received Governor 's Award for Community Service, 1999

Joe Bunkers
111 Arnold Palmer Drive
Nashville, Tennessee
Telephone, email address

Ongoing Public Relations

From your first golf tournament until you retire, remember that every person you meet is a potential sponsor or client. Take the time to sign autographs and chat with fans. When you play in ProAms remember that your playing partners have spent money to have a great day on the golf course with you. Do your best to ensure that they are not disappointed and when you finish the round, ask for business cards or mailing addresses.

The time you spend writing a thank you note or mailing a Christmas card can make a positive impression on a past ProAm partner, who may in the future be your client or sponsor, and will always be your fan.

Even if you do not pursue golf outings or seek potential sponsors, there are simple things that you can do to enhance your marketability – increasing the chances that tournament organizers will be seeking you. Be friendly at golf tournaments and make yourself available to the press. Do not turn down the opportunity to "play" to the camera, during televised events as long as you can do so without it effecting the more important "play" of your golf game.

And if you have an additional talent or have volunteered time for a charitable cause, share that information with the media. The more your name is heard and the more the fans feel they know you, the more a tournament committee wants to see your name in their field.

5.3 Other Team Members

5.3.1 Business Manager and Assistant

It can be easy to be distracted by the paperwork of entering tournaments, filing quarterly taxes, or tracking expenses when your focus should be on practice, rest, physical fitness, and your own mental health. As you concentrate on your game, you may fall behind on record keeping, causing other kinds of problems. The top players – your competition – depend on a business manager and other support staff to help them.

While some players work with one individual who serves as both manager and agent combined, other players hire a manager in a completely separate role than their agent. A manager (also called a business manager) handles the player's schedule, possibly his or her travel arrangements, bill paying, accounting, investment portfolio, and correspondence. A manager sometimes holds a law degree or represents a company with attorneys on staff who specialize in the legal issues of professional athletes.

Some players have also had success by turning the management of their career over to a friend or family member who is appropriately skilled in marketing, law, or finance.

> **HINT:** If you are considering a family member to manage your career, be sure he or she is truly qualified for the role and that the two of you will be able to separate your business relationship from your personal relationship. You can always fire a manager, but you cannot fire them from being your parent, sibling, or spouse.

In addition to a business manager, you may decide at some point to hire a personal assistant. An assistant can help you by running errands, making your travel arrangements, and handling other tasks to free up your time so you can focus on your game.

5.3.2 Your Swing Coach

> **PROBLEM:** You cannot see your own swing and you never get to watch yourself putt.

Although you can solve this problem to some extent by viewing elements of your game on videotape, video has limitations, including the obvious drawback that the tape image is only a two dimensional depiction of a three dimensional action. The best solution is to have a coach.

A good golf coach provides you another set of eyes – trained eyes – studying your swing, your putting, and all details of your game. He or she can see things about you that you have little chance of determining on your own. Even when you are an established player you will probably work with an instructor or a swing coach. After all, you can always be better.

Most professional players work with a swing coach for both long-range improvements and quick fixes. At the top levels of play, if you find a way to improve your game by only one shot per round, the four shot difference per tournament that makes can result in thousands of dollars more in winnings. Also, you will find that your game will vary from time to time. Remember, an unintended tiny change in your grip, stance, or other element of your swing may translate into your ball being many yards off your intended target.

> **EXAMPLE:** Play one tournament in heavy wind. After the first few rounds you will have subconsciously adjusted elements of your swing to compensate for the wind factor. Play the following week in calm weather and suddenly your swing is "out of whack". Perhaps you will be able to adjust again on your own, hopefully before you do too much damage on your scorecard. However, spend 15 minutes under the observant eye of a coach who knows your game and you could be quickly back on track.

Golf coaches typically work with numerous students. Lessons with recreational players, who have much to learn, take up hours of a coach's time. Customarily the student pays for each hour of instruction, even if the coach's assistant rather than the coach teaches it. A professional player needs fewer hours of the coach's time. The pro player's issues are not the mastering of the basics, but typically are the fine-tuning of a skilled game.

Costs

Most golf coaches will charge a fee to teach a professional golfer whose name is not well known. The fee could be less than $100 for a one-hour lesson or could be several thousand dollars for a day of the coach's time. Sometimes a player and a coach negotiate fees, which may be paid monthly, quarterly, or even yearly.

Surprisingly, the agreement may be undefined as to how many lessons, or hours of instruction are included. A few coaches will see such promise in a young pro player that they will teach him or her without charge. And as strange as this may sound – the more successful a player you become, the less you may be expected to pay.

To a golf coach, reputation is important. To publicize that he or she has taught a US Open champion has value that is almost priceless in attracting other students. One of the best ways to repay your golf coach is to acknowledge him by name when you give press interviews after a win or a successful round. Just don't assume that your coach does not also expect a monetary "thank you" as well!

Because fee agreements between coaches and players can vary so greatly, shop around for your coach. Do not hesitate to negotiate for a special or reduced rate. Always make sure that both you and your coach are in complete agreement as to the terms of your arrangement and the rates. Misunderstandings happen easily if one or both of the parties involved made assumptions about what the other expects.

Tips for Selecting Your Coach

- Look for a coach who makes you feel relaxed as you work together.

- Select someone whose swing philosophy is similar to yours. While you may need to make many adjustments in your game, players are rarely successful when they try to scrap their whole approach and learn a new technique.

- Consider who are the other professional players a coach has taught. Are their golfing styles, swing techniques similar to yours? Do his students stay with him or move on?

- If you play left-handed, has this coach worked with other lefties?

- How flexible is his schedule? Will he make adjustments in his other commitments if you find you need an emergency session or his attention during a tournament?

- Does this coach have teaching privileges at a course where you regularly practice? Does he work from a fixed location, such as his teaching center at a golf course? Is this location convenient for you? Does it provide you facilities to work on all aspects of your game or will you be limited to a driving range and a few putting holes only?

Videotaping

In addition to hiring a swing coach, some players invest in video camera equipment and tripods. Others rely on using taping equipment at a golf school or belonging to their golf coach. Taping yourself allows you to study the details of your swing in slow speed and in stop action.

If you use a digital camera for videotaping, or if you have your video transferred to CD-ROM, you can study your swing on most home computers. Special software programs, like the JC Video Personal Golf software are designed for serious golfers who want the ability to track their progress on their personal computer. When it comes to understanding what is going on in your swing, seeing is believing.

JC Video Personal Golf software enables you to play your previously videotaped swing in crystal-clear, frame-by-frame advance, see all the intricate details, compare your swing against a databank of the swings of select pro players or earlier swings of yourself, enter notes about each swing, and easily send your swing image over the Internet. And you don't have to be a computer-whiz to operate the software, thanks to the user-friendly Video Help files included within the program.

The best way to learn more about personal golf software is to visit the websites of leading golf software companies, like:

JC Video Personal Golf Software
www.jcvideo.com

V1 Pro System
www.internetgolfacademy.com

5.3.3 Fitness Trainer

The careers of Tiger Woods and David Duval are testimonies to their belief that fitness training has been essential for pushing their game to a higher level. Gary Player acknowledges weight and flexibility training as key to keeping him injury-free over a career that spans almost fifty years of competitive golf.

It is simple. Assume that half of the players in the next PGA Tour or LPGA Tour event are involved in a regular fitness-training program at a gym or health club. Assume that the other half have personal trainers and are working out in their homes or at private facilities. And assume that if you are not working out, regularly, those other players will probably beat you. It is not a question of if you train and workout as part of your golf routine, it is only a question of how.

Making a Fitness Plan

- See your doctor. Make sure he or she knows you are changing or increasing your fitness routine. Take responsibility for maintaining a healthy heart rate, blood pressure, weight, and cholesterol level.

- Consult a fitness trainer before you begin – even if you intend to work on your own. Plan with your fitness trainer a program that encompasses strength and flexibility.

- Seek someone who understands the needs of a professional golfer and the toll that years of golf take on your back, shoulders, elbows, wrists and other muscles and joints.

- Learn relaxation techniques. Include them in your program.

- Decide whether you can stick to an exercise routine on your own or if you need to work with a personal trainer.

- If you invest in personal exercise equipment, will you be at home enough to justify your investment?

- If you join a health club, does it also have centers you can use in most cities so that you can workout when you are on the road. Do not overlook options like the YMCA, or a church, school or college exercise room that you may be able to use for less money.

- Consider how frequently you stay in hotels with exercise rooms and if their facilities will suit your training needs.

- Do not overlook some simple but effective equipment such as free weights that can be filled with water to use, then emptied for lightweight travel, or elastic bands that provide stretching and resistance but take up almost no room in your suitcase.

- Before you take a life membership in a gym, or sign a long-term contract with a trainer, see if you can pay for a trial period first. Be very cautious if the answer is no. And before you buy expensive equipment, do your research as a consumer. Do not make your purchases on the promises of a salesperson. It may even be worth a short-term membership in a health club to try out similar equipment.

- Lastly, check credentials. Almost anyone with well-developed abs and the right vocabulary can seem as if he or she is educated in fitness training. Your ability to earn a living as a professional athlete is tied to having a strong and healthy body. The wrong exercise, or the right exercise done the wrong way, can wipe out your career if it causes permanent damage. Make sure anyone you are working with is trained and knowledgeable.

HINT: In the US, the National Athletic Trainers' Association (**www.nata.org**) is the organization that provides certification for Athletic Trainers and Therapists. In Canada, it is the Canadian Athletic Therapists Association (**www.athletictherapy.org**). Contact them with your questions about trainers.

For the players on the PGA, Champions, or LPGA Tours, there is an excellent solution to the problem of where to exercise when at a Tour event. HealthSouth, a major healthcare provider and a leader in sports medicine, sends special health and fitness vans to most tournament sites. The use of the facilities and the assistance of the sports medicine experts who staff them, is available to all tournament participants.

Players go to the HealthSouth fitness vans to exercise or spend one-on-one time with a therapist for muscle stretching, strengthening, and conditioning. These mobile workout rooms provide a site that is private and convenient for exercise with properly calibrated and maintained equipment. The staff in the trailers adds the safeguards of their extensive training in sports medicine, fitness, and physical therapy, plus week-to-week familiarity with each player's special needs and training objectives.

Each week as soon as the tournament posts tee times, players hurry to schedule their massage, therapy, or stretching session. They want to be warmed up and ready to play, with the least risk of injury. But just because you are not yet a member of the PGA or LPGA Tours does not mean you can't take advantage of the services of a HealthSouth Golf Professional. The HealthSouth Programs is a resource for golfers of all skill levels, golf teachers, golf coaches, and health professionals, such as clinicians and physicians. It is designed to help the healthy golfer post better scores – and the injured golfer to get back on the course. The HealthSouth Golf Program offers:

• The Golfers Anatomical Analysis, to uncover the deficiencies in strength, flexibility, balance, and range of motion as it pertains to your golf swing. A written evaluation and personalized exercise/flexibility program is provided with the analysis.

• One-hour personal and supervised training sessions can be arranged following the anatomical analysis. Monthly facility use is also available in some locations.

• A nationwide network of more than 300 Certified Golf Specialists trained in golf injury management and prevention, resulting in performance enhancement.

Learn more about the mobile fitness centers used by the pros and the services of HealthSouth available to all golfers at their website at **www.healthsouthgolf.com**.

5.3.4 Sports Psychologist

No one knows who first claimed, "Golf is 90% mental." You hear this quoted often by good players at the end of a bad round. You seldom hear it at the end of a good round – players like to credit a good round to their skill and playing abilities.

Obviously, no one knows the percentages – the formula – to produce a winning game. Part skill, part strategy, part confidence, experience, and luck. Success in golf is mysterious. Sometimes you can see it. Occasionally you get to touch it, but few hold on to it for long.

Training for the mental side of sports competition is crucial. Bookstore and library shelves are stocked with titles that promise to give you the competitive edge, power position, or winning strategy. You can learn a great deal about the different mental approaches to tournament golf just by reading some of the writings of recent years.

And the best part is that they all work. That's right. Every system for improving a player's performance through mind training, mind conditioning, or counseling, works for someone. The catch is, which approach will help you?

Objectives of Many Sports Psychologists

1. The professional player must learn to identify obstacles that are standing in the way of success. Obstacles can take the form of the tangible, such as using equipment that is not suited to the playing style of the player. Intangible obstacles are problems like silently panicking over each shot. Before you can resolve what is preventing you from improving in your game, you must be able to identify it. Often, it will be multiple reasons, both tangible and intangible.

2. Players need a pre-shot routine as a way to focus his or her thoughts. A routine enables the player, no matter how nervous or how pressured, to lapse into a comfortable, familiar habit – something done so frequently it is second nature. A routine decreases stress and increases the odds of hitting consistent, predictable shots.

3. The player must also develop mental cues to help force him or her to play one shot at a time. A golfer whose mind is rampaging ahead to the difficult shot to be faced on the next hole, will never give proper attention to the shot currently being played. Sports psychologists try to help a player learn how to stay in the moment.

Some of what you learn from sports psychologists may be enlightening to you. The techniques they teach you can be a tremendous help to keep you focused. Other "secrets" you learn from a sports psychologist might seem to you to be only common sense. But, ask any player who has just won a tournament after applying techniques learned from a sports psychologist, they will tell you that whatever the fee – they were glad they invested in the help.

5.3.5 Caddie

A caddie is an independent contractor hired by a golfer to provide caddie service during play and usually during practice. The player-caddie work arrangement may be for a single tournament, a series of tournaments or for a playing season.

Sometimes a caddie who regularly works at the tournament golf course will "pick up a bag" (a golfing expression for accepting a job as a caddie). Players call these caddies *local caddies*. A local caddie typically caddies only at that golf course, usually for recreational players.

If a professional tournament is held there, the local caddie may get a caddying job for the tournament by being at the golf course (or at the Monday Qualifying site) and approaching players as they arrive. A player who perhaps did not anticipate playing in a tournament may arrive at the last minute and ask the club pro or Caddiemaster to recommend a local caddie.

Some players seek a local caddie because he or she is likely to know the ins and outs of that golf course particularly well, and is sometimes so enthusiastic to have the opportunity to work for a professional golfer that he accepts lower than average pay.

Most of the caddies who work for players on the main tours are tour caddies, and travel the tournament circuit, like the players. A tour caddie may have a written or verbal contract to work for a player, but many tour caddies do not. Without an agreement with a player, a tour caddie will travel to a tournament and hope to be hired. Caddies simply approach players outside the locker room or on the practice range and offer their services for the week. A tour caddie is always looking for a player who plays regularly and wins large checks.

Currently there is not a union for caddies, but there are caddie associations. And while there are no specific standardizations for the skills of a caddie, you can be sure, that the proficiency most players expect from their caddies is very high.

Top professional players frequently prefer to work with the same caddie week after week. These players pay their caddie well to ensure that he or she works exclusively for them. After all, a good caddie rarely improves a player's game, but a poor caddie can be costly.

Typically, a caddie bears the expense of his or her own travel, housing, and food. Caddies usually try to do this at the lowest possible costs to increase the earnings they realize each week.

There are many different types of relationships between players and their caddies. Some players turn to their caddie as a friend, while others keep the player-caddie relationship all business. A few players look to their caddie for moral and psychological support during play. Others may expect their caddie to be a coach, a cheerleader or even a comedian to break the tension of tournament competition.

A player may want the caddie to simply clean the clubs and balls during play, repair divots, and keep quiet. Players and caddies call this, "keep up and shut up." Most professional players, at least, consult their caddie on yardages, the line of the putt and club selection. How often they actually take their caddies' advice is something only the player and the caddie know for sure.

The minimum payment an experienced tour caddie typically accepts is roughly $700 per week plus 5% of the player's winnings for that tournament. Many players pay their caddies $900-$1,000 per week. The bonus percentage can be as high as 10% of the player's winnings. Other players simply negotiate to pay their caddie an annual salary. A caddie on the Nationwide Tour, where tournament purses are smaller, may work for as little as $400 per week and no bonus payment.

As 14-time PGA Tour winner Hal Sutton said in February 2001, in an Associated Press interview, "other than being with your wife, you have no closer relationship with anybody than your caddie. . ." Interestingly, Sutton has fired and re-hired the same caddie three times during his 20-year career.

> **HINT:** For one of the best learning experiences about life as a professional golfer, consider spending a season as a tournament caddie. You will not make much money as a beginning caddie, but the education will be incredibly valuable.

6. The Game of Life

6.1 If Life Takes You Off Course

The lens of a television camera filters the view the world sees of most professional golfers. Don't assume because you only see them celebrating in the winner's circle, that life always gives pro golfers reasons to smile. Million dollar winnings and your name in the record books solve many problems, but it does not insulate you from personal challenges. The difference in being a champion, off the course or on, becomes how you choose to handle life's adversities.

The playing career of Paul Azinger, winner of the PGA Championship and at that time 11 other PGA tournaments, came abruptly to a standstill in 1993. Azinger was ill. The diagnosis was cancer – lymphoma in his right shoulder. The following year, lean and bald from chemotherapy, he played only four regular season PGA Tour events. Twice he missed the cut.

Azinger joked with the other players about his strong stomach muscles from so much time spent throwing up, yet he silently suffered, fearing he had lost his ability to ever win again. For much of the five years that followed, Azinger struggled. He was winless and missed the cut in one out of every three tournaments he entered.

But Paul Azinger didn't give up. In January 2000, he picked up a $522,000 check and the winner's trophy at the Sony Open in Hawaii. He played 38 events over the 2000 and 2001 seasons. He only missed the cut twice. In the 2002 season, Azinger added two more PGA Tour top-ten finishes to his stats, including 4th place at the WGC-Accenture Match Play Championship.

Paul Azinger is only one of many golfers who have overcome adversity to achieve their dreams. Diabetics Michelle McGann, Sherri Turner, and Kellie Kuehne all play every LPGA event linked to personal insulin pumps. Between them, they have nine tournament wins.

Professional golfer Sung Man Lee has never heard the cheer of the gallery or even the satisfying plop of his ball in the hole. The crowd is applauding and his ball is definitely going in, but Sung Man Lee who is almost totally deaf, plays without ever hearing the sounds of the game. Korean born Sung Man Lee played the Nationwide Tour in 2001. He was not yet 21 years old.

Many successful golfers have triumphed over illness, injuries, loss of loved ones, and other adversity. Billy Glasson, with a medical history including one elbow surgery, four sinus operations, four knee surgeries, one lip surgery, and one arm surgery is practically the PGA Tour's poster boy for their health insurance plan. The PGA Tour voted Glasson Comeback Player of the Year, when he won the 1997 Las Vegas Invitational after surgery the previous year for a detached shoulder muscle.

These are just a few of golf's stories of personal triumph. There are certainly many more. All professional players face challenges whether they are playing well or struggling to earn their spot on a tour.

Some emerge as true champions. They do so because they have learned to finish the round with their head held high, even when they are the last player in the field. They recognize that wins and losses on the golf course are in fact, only parts of a game. And most importantly, when serious misfortune does occur, they face it as if it is the ultimate play-off and they intend to accept nothing less than the win.

6.2 You're in the Clubhouse Now

Becoming a successful professional golfer will not be easy. But if you have skill, determination, and desire to play the game professionally, you may be the right person to give golf a serious try. Take the tips you have learned in this guide and back them up with hours of practice. Make a plan for your life and a back-up plan, then approach the game, one hole at a time.

In 1969, professional golfer Orville Moody was on the 35th hole of a 36-hole qualifier for the US Open. It was a strength–sapping Dallas day in June, and Moody had already played 34 holes since teeing off that morning a little past nine. Word came back to him from a caddie that he would need to shoot a birdie and at least a par on the last two holes to make it into the tournament. But things did not look good for Moody.

He hit his approach shot on the next-to-the-last hole. It landed in a deep bunker left of the green. The lie was bad, the shot it left him was worse. Moody looked at his sweaty playing partner in annoyance – this guy was two under and would easily qualify. Angry, tired, and ready to give in, Moody climbed into the trap, ready to slap the ball and bring his misery to a quick end. But he paused.

He took a deep breath. Perhaps he remembered that this was the career he had planned. So he stepped out of the bunker and studied the shot. An earthy mound blocked all view of the hole, but past it, he saw that the green sloped to water on the back and a guaranteed double bogey on the right. It was worse than he even expected. He'd have to land his ball on a strip of fringe not more than 18 inches wide, putt, and save par, then hope to birdie 18.

Moody hit a bunker shot that might have been his best effort ever. Gently his ball hit the fringe, and then it started to roll. It traveled in an arcing line, 30 feet to the hole, and dropped in. Moody followed this impossible birdie with a par on his last hole to claim the last spot in the US Open Qualifier.

Golf does not come with any promises, but you never know which shot may change your life. Ask Orville Moody, winner of the 1969 US Open.

So square your feet, take aim, and give it your best. After all, you may be the PGA Tour's next Rookie of the Year.

7. Resource Section

7.1 Golf Definitions

The game of golf definitely has a language all it's own. The definitions listed below are only some of the many words you will need to know and understand if you plan to 'walk the walk and talk the talk.' In addition to making sure you understand all of the words listed here, open up your copy of the USGA *Rules of Golf* and learn exactly how the United States Golf Association and the Royal and Ancient define many terms commonly used and misused by golfers.

Balance Point
The place on a club shaft where the golf club's weight is evenly distributed in either direction.

Birdie
The name for the score on any hole played in one shot less than the score that has been established as par for that hole.

Bogey
The name for the score on any hole played in one shot more than the score that has been established as par for that hole. Playing a hole in two shots more than the score that has been established as par for that hole is called a double bogey.

Cut
The reduction of the playing field in a tournament, occurring after a pre-set number of rounds of play (most typically two rounds). Tournament cuts often follow the criteria of reducing the number of players to any of the following: Any player within ten shots of the score of the currently leading player, either the lowest scoring 50, 60, or 70 players and respectively anyone tied with the score of the 50th, 60th, or 70th player.

Draw
The grouping of players and their assignment to a tee time is called the draw. The draw follows a formula based on previous performance for tournaments on some golf tours, and is made randomly for tournaments on other tours.

Drive	A golf shot hit off the tee with the driver, typically the longest club in the bag. A shot hit off the tee with any club other than the driver is a tee shot.
Eagle	The name for the score on any hole played in two shots less than the score that has been established as par for that hole.
Executive Golf Course	May be either a 9-hole or and an 18-hole course, although most frequently is a 9-hole course. Will offer a variety of par three, par four and par five holes.
Fairway	The closely mown areas of the golf course, between the tee and the green. The USGA's Rules of Golf does not use the word fairway in discussion of play; but instead says, "through the green".
Flex	The bending property in a golf club shaft. Club manufacturers use different names to define the flex within a shaft, but some of the most common classifications include: "L" for Ladies, "R" for Regular, "S" for Stiff and "X" for Extra Stiff, sometimes called Tour Pro.
Gallery	The spectators at a golf tournament or golf event.
Golf Ball	A ball which is not larger than 1.680 inches; does not weigh more than 1.62 ounces and conforms to standards of acceptability as established by the USGA and the Royal and Ancient.
Grip	The word grip in golf can refer to either: (a) a player's hand positioning on the club, including the tightness or looseness in the way he or she is holding his hands around the club handle, or (b) the rubber, leather or vinyl covering that wraps the butt end of a club shaft.
Hook	A golf shot that veers left of the intended target when hit by a right handed player or right of the intended target when hit by a left handed player. This shot may be hit deliberately or in error.
Junior Golfer	Typically considered any golfer under the age of 18; some criteria include the requirement that a Junior Golfer is additionally, over the age of 4.

Lie	The word lie in golf can refer to either: (a) the angle of the club shaft in relation to the sole of the club, or (b) the resting place of a golf ball in play.
Loft	The measurement by degrees of the clubface angle relative to the club shaft.
Match Play	In Match Play the game is played hole by hole, with competition being either one on one or team against team. The individual or team who attains the lowest score (fewest number of strokes) on a hole is said to "win" that hole. The individual or team leading the match with the lowest score is said to be "holes up" by the number of holes that he leads. If the individuals or teams competing are tied, have "won" equal number of holes, then the match is said to be, "all square". When an individual or a side has as many holes to be played as they are then "up", they are said to be "dormie".
Par-Three Course	A par-three course has only par three golf holes and each hole typically averages 100 yards in length. In some areas of the country, this is called a Pitch and Putt course.
Pin	The flagstick used to indicate hole placement on the green.
Pitch	A short, lofted golf shot.
Purse	The total amount of money for which players compete in a tournament.
Putt	A golf stroke made with a putter.
Regulation Golf Course	May be either a nine-hole or an eighteen-hole course that is comprised of par three, par four, and par five holes. If it is a nine-hole course, it must be at least 2,600 yards in length and at least par 33. If it is an eighteen-hole course, it must be at least 5,200 yards in length and at least par 66.
Top	A mis-hit shot where the club's point of impact with the ball is above the "equator" of the ball.

7.2 Books

There are many excellent books available to learn more about the topics discussed in this guide, including:

- *8 Traits of Champion Golfers*, by Dr. Deborah Graham and Jon Stabler

- *A Golfer's Life*, by Arnold Palmer with James Dodson

- *A Good Walk Spoiled, Days and Nights on the PGA Tour,* by John Feinsten

- *American Golf Courses: American's Most Challenging Public Golf Courses*, by Jim Moriarty and Robert Trent Jones

- *Athlete's Guide to Agents*, by Robert H. Ruxin and Gary Uberstine

- *Bury Me in a Pot Bunker*, by Pete Dye and Mark Shaw

- *Byron Nelson: The Little Black Book,* by Byron Nelson

- *Eat That Frog! 21 Great Ways to Stop Procrastinating and Get More Done in Less Time*, by Brian Tracy

- *Ernie El's Guide to Golf Fitness: Take Strokes Off Your Game and Add Yards to Your Drives*, by Ernie Els and David Herman

- *From the Prom to the Pros: The Athlete's, Parent's, and Coach's Guide*, by David Allen Smith

- *The Game I Love*, by Sam Snead with Fran Pirozzolo

- *Golf Begins at 50: Playing the Lifetime Game Better than Ever,* by Gary Player and Desmond Tolhurst

- *Golf Course Designs*, by Tom Fazio

- *Golf is a Game of Confidence*, by Robert J. Rotella, et. al

- *Golf Rules Plain and Simple*, by Mark Russell

- *Life is Not a Game of Perfect: Finding Your Real Talent and Making it Work for You*, by Robert J. Rotella, et. al

- *The Majors: In Pursuit of Golf's Holy Grail*, by John Feinstein

- *The Masters: Golf, Money, and Power in Augusta, Georgia*, by Curt Sampson

- *The Methods of Golf's Masters: How They Played and What You Can Learn From Them*, by Dick Aultman, Ken Bowden, and Herbert Warren Wind.

- *The Psychology of Tournament Golf*, by David L.Cook Ph.D.

- *Zinger: A Champion's Story of Determination, Courage, and Charging Back*, by Paul Azinger and Ken Abraham

See the other side for a special offer coupon.

See the other side for a special offer coupon.

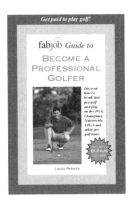

See the other side for a special offer coupon.

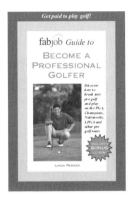

See the other side for a special offer coupon.

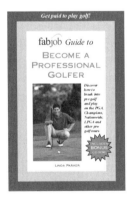

Also From FabJob.com

As a motivational speaker you can earn applause and admiration, plus up to thousands of dollars every time you speak. Read the *FabJob Guide to Become a Motivational Speaker* to discover how you can get hired as a motivational speaker, seminar presenter, trainer, or adult education instructor. Also includes step-by-step advice on how to start your own profitable business presenting seminars.

Order Become a Motivational Speaker
or dozens of other career guides
at www.FabJob.com

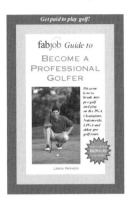